Andrew M Jones

The Innovation Acid Test

Growth Through Design and Differentiation

D1494125

Published by:
Triarchy Press
Station Offices
Station Yard
Axminster EX13 5PF
United Kingdom

+44 (0)1297 631456
info@triarchypress.com
www.triarchypress.com

First Published 2008

Cover design and identity by:
Bond and Coyne Associates Ltd

ISBN: 978-0-9550081-5-3

Contents

Acknowledgements   vii

Foreword - Keith Grint   viii

1   Introduction   11

     1.1 Innovation and the Human-Centred Enterprise   11
     1.2 A Thousand Flowers Innovating   12
     1.3 The Human-Centred Enterprise   14
     1.4 Drucker's Maxim   17
     1.5 From 'Managing the Known' to 'Building the Unknown'   18
     1.6 The 'Design Revolution'   20
     1.7 Outline of the Book   26

2   Architecture and the 'Timeless Way of Building' at SAS   27

     2.1 Christopher Alexander   27
     2.2 Cultural Architecture and 'Human-Centred Management' at SAS   30
     2.3 SAS's Human-Centred-Enterprise Commitments   32
     2.4 Human-Centred 'Pattern Languages' at SAS   41

3   Innovation by Design   43

     3.1 What is Design?   43
     3.2 Elevating Design   45
     3.3 Innovation at GE   47
     3.4 P&G   48
     3.5 Customer Immersion at Credit Suisse   51
     3.6 IDEO and Bank of America   53
     3.7 'Business Design' Education and T-Shaped Recruits   55
     3.8 Stanford's d-school: The Hasso Plattner Institute of Design   56

3.9 IIT Institute of Design   58

3.10 Rotman School of Management (University of Toronto)   60

4   Anthropology and Innovation   62

4.1 What is Ethnography?   62

4.2 Ethnography at Intel   63

4.3 Ethnography at Microsoft   66

4.4 Ethnographic Praxis in Industry Conference (EPIC), 2005-2006   68

4.5 Ethnographic Consultancies   69

4.6 Peter Drucker, Consumer Anthropology and Innovation   70

5   Employees First: Cultural Innovation at Southwest Airlines   74

5.1 Low Budget Airlines   74

5.2 Tangible Commitments, Not Platitudes   78

5.3 Recruiting Happiness   79

5.4 Empathy and Organizational Learning   80

5.5 Great Service Begins at Home   83

5.6 The Pattern Languages of Southwest Airlines   87

6   'It's All Teams at Whole Foods'   90

6.1 Creator and Driver   90

6.2 Innovation, Creativity and Theatre at Whole Foods   91

6.3 Growing Up   93

6.4 'Whole Foods is All Teams'   94

6.5 John Mackey on 'Control'   99

6.6 The New Pragmatism   101

7   Stimulating Customer Experience at Starbucks   104

7.1 Café Culture   104

7.2 Coffee in the US and Britain   104

7.3 Enter Starbucks   105

7.4 Innovation at Starbucks 107

7.5 Starbucks Office 108

7.6 Starbucks Music 109

7.7 Starbucks Media 114

7.8 Internal Innovation at Starbucks 116

7.9 Customer Experience Rules 119

7.10 Starbucks's Virtuous Spiral 120

7.11 Schultz's Memo 120

8 Google and All the Information in the World 122

8.1 Über-Innovator 122

8.2 Boons not Bombs 123

8.3 GoogleWare and the Google Economy 125

8.4 GoogleVation 128

8.5 Back on Campus 130

8.6 Sharethewealth.com 134

8.7 GooglePharma 137

9 One Hundred Per Cent Innocent 139

9.1 105 Per Cent Innocent 139

9.2 Should We Quit Our Jobs? 140

9.3 Drucker's Innocence 142

9.4 The Cause 145

9.5 Fruitstock 147

10 'Designed in China' by Shanghai Tang 149

10.1 To Return to Innovation by Design 149

10.2 Designed in China 150

10.3 The Anthropology of Innovation at Shanghai Tang 152

11 Innovating in a Theory X World 157

11.1 X and Y Views   157

11.2 Leading by Design   160

11.3 An Innovative Culture is an Engaged Culture   162

11.4 A Methodology for Building HCEs   165

Glossary   172

Notes   181

About Triarchy Press   194

About the Author   195

Acknowledgements

Several particular individuals have been instrumental in the development of my thinking and writing. First, Roger McConochie, one of the pioneers of Business Anthropology, has been a mentor, inspiration and dear friend for many years. He helped me see that culture resides in the here and now, that it is in business as much as in remote tribes in far away places. My life has been an extended field project since that chance meeting at the Baltimore-Washington Airport in 1995.

Secondly, Alfred Werner, Über-Technologist and life-strategist, introduced me to a design-centred view of life and its possibilities. He suggested that I read Christopher Alexander's *The Timeless Way of Building*, which has influenced everything I've done since. He helped me see that life is a design process, and that planning is not living.

I am very grateful for the opportunity to spread my wings in the UK under the leadership of David Collinson and Keith Grint at Lancaster University Management School. The chance to work with two scholars at the very top of the field has raised the bar in rather intimidating ways. I hope not to disappoint.

Also, to my good friend Dr Peter Lenney of Lancaster University Management School, that rare beast who has done it all - thanks! Your clear and deep thinking has helped shape and focus the thinking and writing that resulted in this book more than you know. See you at the Taps at 9:00!

A huge thank you to Andrew Carey and Huw Hennessy for editing the manuscript. Special thanks to Andrew, who did the heavy lifting. As a first time book author, I did not realize just how critical and valuable good editing is to the final read of a book. Andrew's name should be on the front cover of the book - thanks!

Finally, and most importantly, an unlimited thanks to Jean Sulzby Jones, my better half for almost twenty years, and to our little sprockets: Mae, Christopher and Stuart. Without love there is no reason to bother with any of this.

Foreword - Keith Grint

The quest for the holy grail of innovation

The quest for the holy grail of innovation resembles that very same mythical journey: each time the vision appears on the jacket of a new book, disciples rush to consume the contents - and usually wait for the indigestion to set in. Drew Jones doesn't promise a holy grail, primarily because there isn't one, but he provides enough knowledge, clues and experiences for even the most cynical executive to rethink their approach to innovation. Eschewing the usual psychological path to the treasure, Jones insists that we try his anthropological mantle instead. Rather than analysing why individuals seem so resistant to 'rational' policies for innovation, Jones illustrates the value of copying anthropological methodology: i.e. living amongst tribes in order to improve understanding of their cultures. If, as now seems certain, most sustainable change and innovation requires cultural change not simply psychological redirection, then this alternative path has to lead us in the right direction. Indeed, each of the cases that Jones examines resonates with a similar organizational premise: relying on formal leaders or specialized innovation units is not the way to long term success. Thus, just as Toyota's success is rooted in a cultural norm of *innovation by all,* so too is that of the cases Jones considers: Starbucks, Whole Foods, Southwest Airlines, Google, Innocent Drinks and Shanghai Tang.

The switch from *heuristics* to *algorithms,* which Jones suggests typifies the organizational journey of most companies in the 20th century, is now being replaced by a move towards human-centred design heuristics where innovation becomes the framing architecture. Architecture provides frames and, by extension, also the spaces within the frames wherein innovation takes place. Perhaps we can turn to the Tao to understand this metaphor better:

Tao De Ching Verse 11

Thirty spokes share the wheel's hub;
It is the centre hole that makes it useful.
Shape clay into a vessel;
It is the space within that makes it useful.
Cut doors and windows for a room;
It is the holes which make it useful.
Therefore profit comes from what is there;
Usefulness from what is not there.

Jones' point is that unless we design our organizations to facilitate human interaction - the basis for innovation - we will remain stuck with a division of labour that means mundane work for most and a consequential inertia that inhibits rather than encourages change. In contrast, the case studies selected speak of this other strange world where workers are free to enjoy work, to take control of their own lives and to engage in the innovation that most anxious CEOs can only dream of. Thus SAS Institute insists on just a 7 hour day so that family life is not sacrificed for 'the company'. This is not motherhood and apple pie land but hard nosed economic rationality because this company's retention rate is amongst the highest in its industry and the consequence is that discretionary effort by employees becomes the source of innovation. Similarly, the rise and rise of Wholefoods is not down to their rose-tinted view of supportive teamwork in their stores - this is not 1968 but 2008. It is the ruthless competition that teams engage in - their shared fate - that generates the urge to innovate. And while Google remains amongst the most innovative of all companies, and one of the most popular to work for, the connection between these two statements is not coincidental. At Google, twenty per cent of an employee's time can be devoted to a pet innovation project, not because each project promises a strong return on investment, but because there is a systemic commitment to staff matters and the company recognizes that oftentimes the greatest innovations occur through private play rather than collective discipline.

However, the radical nature of these alternative organizations is not simply embodied in the organizational architecture but also in their innovative practices, which are often rooted in empathy. Hence, many of the design innovations mentioned are derived from employees working with customers to understand users' requirements. This anthropological method - living amongst people to understand them better - also involves senior executives returning to the shop floor at regular intervals to reacquaint themselves with reality at the sharp end. In each of the companies, management is 'Walking a mile in someone else's shoes', either as bank customers at Credit Suisse or BoA or coffee drinkers at Starbucks or IT users at the home of Intel customers. Traditionally, if organizations want user/customer feedback they employ focus groups or commission surveys but neither of these approaches creates the 'thick descriptions' beloved of anthropologists and, more importantly here, they generally fail to stimulate much innovation. Indeed, therein lies a profoundly important aspect of Jones' self-reflective argument: if you want innovation you have to be innovative. But *being innovative* does not mean employing hugely expensive consultancy teams to dream up hugely expensive dependency regimes. Instead it simply means doing what should come naturally: understanding what consumers normally do in their normal modes of existence and using this information as the springboard to innovation. To put it another way, as Drucker insisted, we cannot be reliant on mavericks and resisters to be constructively innovative - that has to be the responsibility of everyone.

If that is the basis for radical innovation then organizations need to follow the commitment priorities of Southwest Airlines: put your staff first and they will be committed to your customers who will satisfy your shareholders. If, as happens in most organizations, the order is reversed you should not be surprised to find your staff's lack of innovative spirit: if you don't care about them why should they care about you?

So, to the bottom line: will Jones' book make your company more innovative and successful? That depends on you. Many auto executives from the outside have observed how Toyota excel at producing cars by engaging their whole staff in the process of innovation - but few of them manage to replicate that knowledge back in their own plants. Why? Perhaps because radical change threatens to destabilize conventional hierarchies of power and reward. After all, those private and personal management perks and privileges are rather pleasant and it would be a shame to lose some of these just for the sake of creating a world-beating innovative company that works for everyone - wouldn't it?

Keith Grint

Professor of Defence Leadership & Deputy Principal (Management and Leadership)
Defence Leadership & Management Centre
Defence College of Management and Technology
Cranfield University

Email: kgrint.cu@defenceacademy.mod.uk
Leadership journal homepage: http://lea.sagepub.com/

1 Introduction

1.1 Innovation and the Human-Centred Enterprise

Over recent years *innovation* and *internal organic growth* have climbed to the top of the corporate agenda. Recent studies on the importance of innovation, as well as anecdotal evidence, now suggest that today's global business environment is in some respects a 'post-execution' environment. For the past several years management gurus have extolled the virtues of execution as if *what* needs to be executed is no longer in question. This assumes that corporate strategy is clear and fixed and that employees have little to do but turn up and follow orders. While execution is and always will be important for firms, it is no longer enough on its own.

Management gurus have extolled the virtues of execution as if *what* needs to be executed is no longer in question.

New ideas, from both employees and customers, often redirect corporate strategy in productive ways. Companies such as Toyota, BMW and Southwest Airlines regularly incorporate fresh ideas from employees and customers and in doing so their strategic goals gradually change over time. That is, in these companies employees do not simply 'execute' mindlessly. They are empowered to make real decisions in real time that matter to the future of the company. In this respect, they are working in 'post-execution' workplaces. On the one hand, employee creativity and innovation are talked about as being important strategic activities and goals. On the other hand, businesses and business schools still treat innovation as an exceptional feature of business life and as an elective in the majority of MBA programmes throughout the world. In firms that actually solicit and incorporate employee insight into work processes, 'execution' is a fluid and evolving concept and not a simple set of marching orders.

Businesses and business schools still treat innovation as an exceptional feature of business life and as an elective in the majority of MBA programmes.

Take for example the October 2006 issue of *Harvard Business Review*, in which David Garvin and Lynne Levesque further extend this view of 'innovation as an exception'. The article concerns the challenges of 'corporate entrepreneurship' and in it they argue that 'new businesses require innovation, innovation requires fresh ideas, and fresh ideas require mavericks… But most mavericks, sadly, can't tell the difference between good and bad ideas'. Then, as if to validate this myopic view of human creativity, they quote former Home Depot CEO (and current Chrysler CEO), Robert Nardelli, when he says: '[T]here's only a fine line between entrepreneurship and insubordination'.

If innovation is increasingly important to business leaders, as they say it is, while at the same time it is seen as an activity engaged in by mavericks and insubordinates, then what type of serious commitment and investment are companies likely to give to an innovation agenda? The answer, sadly, is not very much. The gap between the rhetoric surrounding the importance of innovation and tangible commitments to innovation as an integral part of business strategy can sometimes be enormous.

> The gap between the rhetoric surrounding the importance of innovation and tangible commitments to innovation as an integral part of business strategy can sometimes be enormous.

1.2   A Thousand Flowers Innovating

This book is about that gap. I am interested in an alternative perspective, one that sits opposite the dominant 'innovation as insubordination' view of the world. This perspective, embraced in different ways by the seven firms considered here - Southwest Airlines, Google, Whole Foods, SAS Institute, Starbucks, Innocent Drinks and Shanghai Tang - views innovation as an everyday organizing principle of work itself. This applies to work within a company, as well as to the process by which new products, services and experiences are delivered to customers. In this book I adopt a broad definition of

Getting new ideas into practice is one of the most difficult challenges facing would-be innovators.

innovation, one borrowed from IDEO's Tom Kelley. Kelley defines innovation simply as 'people generating value through the implementation of new ideas'. This sounds simple, but getting new ideas into practice is, as those who have tried can attest, one of the most difficult challenges facing would-be innovators.

Consider Germany's BMW, which expects employees at all levels of the company to generate new ideas to push the company further into an innovative future. Some of their most innovative features and design concepts are derived from line-level engineers who are encouraged to insert their own ideas into the design and manufacturing process at the company. They are not viewed as mavericks or as insubordinates; they are simply employees. At BMW innovation is everyone's business and the traditional view that innovative strategy is generated at the board level and employees are there simply to execute is challenged on a daily basis. Yet, as its financial results and global cultural equity among consumers indicate, BMW is successful in what it does. It is, like the firms I shall discuss in more detail, 'subversive' as well as successful. Similarly, at Toyota, the notion of *many flowers blooming* is taken even further. Each year hundreds of thousands of employee ideas for process improvement are incorporated into the company's day-to-day work. Toyota too has the financial heft to prove that this translates into success. As I elaborate throughout the book, it will become clear that these organizations are successful precisely because they dare to be different and have the courage to innovate.

Not all firms, of course, can be as creative and innovative as these high flyers. However, an increasing number of traditional 'old-school' firms - Procter & Gamble (P&G), General Electric (GE), Kimberly Clarke, Unilever, Pitney Bowes, Office Max, Whirlpool and HP - have begun to embrace some of the emerging *disciplines of innovation*, such as *design* and *design thinking*, *architecture* and

Ethnography, architecture
and design together form
the emerging disciplines
of innovation that are
being integrated into the
organizational DNA of a new
breed of innovative firms.

ethnography. Ethnography, architecture and design together form the emerging *disciplines of innovation* that are being integrated into the organizational DNA of a new breed of innovative firms; firms both old and new. While the case studies I present here are intended as examples and exemplars of financially successful firms that were founded in an ethos and culture of innovation, each company accomplishes this in a different way. Innovation discipline in some instances is largely implicit. Some of these firms are so grounded in innovation that they no longer have to talk about it; they 'just do it'. Other firms, in fact most of the companies in the world, have to work hard at this. Hopefully, this book can prove useful for those companies contemplating the journey to innovation. More specifically, I am interested in advancing the notion of human-centred innovation, as it is increasingly referred to by design firms engaged in helping firms increase innovative capacity. What, though, do human-centred innovation and human-centred design mean?

1.3   The Human-Centred Enterprise

The award-winning design and innovation consultancy, IDEO, refers to its work as 'human-centred' design and innovation. This is the spirit I try to capture here. The human-centred enterprise (HCE) as a management concept is drawn from the vocabulary of user-centred design, as it manifests itself in the work of architects, computer programmers, industrial designers, urban designers and 'consumer-experience' designers. This book is presented with attitude: it is loudly and equally focused on the principles of humanistic management and consumer-focused innovation. Of course, others, such as Roger Martin, Bruce Nussbaum, Tom Kelley, Herbert Simon, Daniel Pink, Jeffrey Pfeffer, Tim Brown, Fred Collopy, Richard Boland and above all, Peter Drucker, have written about many of these ideas for years, but I believe this book brings together their ideas in a way that can reshape our approach to innovation.

If the *Cluetrain Manifesto* was intended to start a conversation, then this book hopes to extend that conversation. Here I synthesize and chronicle what I see as a cultural shift occurring in the way that some businesses are thinking and working. Keywords and key phrases in an emergent, innovation-oriented management agenda are: differentiation; consumer experience and experience design; employee experience and experience design; ethnography; prototyping; iterative and abductive work; experimentation and sustainable business practice.

A central idealism defines the '*Fast Company* generation' that I write about here. In his Foreward [sic] to the recently published, edited volume of *Fast Company* articles, Jim Collins (co-author of *Built to Last* and *Good to Great*) sums up these values and goals succinctly in the following observations and subsequent 'five basic premises':

> The point - that we should think about life, work, and the connection between the two - needs to be resuscitated. Sifting through the best articles from *Fast Company*'s first ten years, I see an underlying order to the chaos, captured in five basic premises that - while the bubble has come and gone - remain relevant:
>
> *Premise No. 1: Work is not a means to an end; it is an end in itself.* If you create work you are deeply passionate about - because you love to do it and you believe in what it can contribute - the very act of work can become a source of sanctuary and meaning.
>
> *Premise No. 2: If your competitive scorecard is money, you will always lose.* There are two ways to be wealthy. One is to have a

huge amount of money. The other is to have simple needs. What is your answer to 'How much is enough?' As Professor Michael Ray of Stanford taught: comparison is the primary sin of modern life.

Premise No. 3: Business is a mechanism for social change - for good and ill. If you build a great enterprise, it will have an impact - on its people, on its customers, on the communities it touches. The question is: will that impact be positive? How will the world be better off, beyond wealth creation?

Premise No. 4: Entrepreneurship is a life concept, not a business concept. There are two approaches to life. One is to buy the 'paint-by-numbers kit' and stay within the lines. The other is to start with a blank canvas and try to paint a masterpiece. You can be an entrepreneur without starting a company, by creating a path uniquely designed by you.

Premise No. 5: Performance is the fundamental requirement. Good intentions mean nothing without great performance. Businesses must deliver results. Nonprofits must deliver on mission. People must deliver on responsibilities.

In a nutshell, Jim Collins is introducing us to some of the core values and commitments of what I describe as a New Pragmatism that is evolving within the business community in countries such as the UK and the US. When Al Gore announced in the summer of 2007 that he would not make another run for the US Presidency, he stated in *Fast Company* magazine that much of

Much of the progressive agenda in the West - green and clean technology, sustainable enterprises, socially responsible investment funds - is actually being led by business and not government.

the progressive agenda in the West - green and clean technology, sustainable enterprises, socially responsible investment funds - is actually being led by business and not government. That is, the social idealism that originated in the 1960s and 1970s is alive today in the business community more so than it is in many governments throughout the world. Among participants in this business-cultural movement, if one can call it that, the goals of profit and social good are not seen as incompatible. In some respects this *is* reflected in politics, in notions such as the Third Way in British politics and in President Clinton's business-friendly management of the Democratic Party in the US.

1.4   Drucker's Maxim

Peter Drucker has been enormously influential in the world of management, challenging two generations of managers to ask such basic questions as: 'what business am I in?'; 'who is my real customer?' and 'if I was not in this business already, would I go into it today?'. He is famous for saying that he never gave advice so much as he asked good questions. Nevertheless, he did give advice, often in grand claims and proclamations. One of his core insights, which I believe is as fundamental and true today as it was in the early 1970s when he first wrote about it, concerns where and how 'value' is created in firms and where it is lost. He made some of his most important and timeless statements in his 1973 textbook, *Management: Tasks, Responsibilities, Practices.*

The first of these statements is that 'the purpose of a business is to create a customer'. Drucker suggested that:

'The purpose of a business is to create a customer'.

'Because its purpose is to create a customer, the business enterprise has two - and only these two - basic functions: marketing and innovation. Marketing and innovation produce results; all the rest are costs'. Continuing, he says it is necessary that 'business starts out with the needs, the realities, the values of the customer... business [must] define its goal as the satisfaction of customer needs... business [must] base its reward on its contribution to the customer'. Give or take a few different words here or there, these sentences could easily have been written by one of today's design enthusiasts discussing the importance of customer experience in the 'experience economy'. Distilled, Drucker offers a simple formula here, where he suggests that Results are derived from Marketing and Innovation and that all else represents costs: $I + M = R$. I prefer to present the formula as $I + M = V$ (Value). This is, as I suggest throughout the book, the *modus operandi* of today's design and innovation consultancies, as well as of design- and innovation-focused large firms. Drucker was years ahead of his time and the bulk of the argument I am making here, and that others like Bruce Nussbaum at *Business Week* and Roger Martin at the Rotman School of Management are making today, draw closely on Drucker's thinking. For Drucker, innovation was not for mavericks and insubordinates, but rather it was the purpose of business itself. Firms like those profiled in this book make this a reality every day. And a goal of this book is to try to reclaim the simple Drucker maxim that *the purpose of a business is to innovate for customer experience* (and not to play the quarterly earnings game on behalf of institutional investors, to get inflated media coverage or to inflate short-term share prices for the sake of executive compensation or anything else). Simple stuff, but nevertheless true.

> For Drucker, innovation was not for mavericks and insubordinates, it was the purpose of business itself.

1.5   From 'Managing the Known' to 'Building the Unknown'

How, though, do you get to innovation? How do you break out of the frameworks of thinking and practice that prevent mainstream managers from understanding and appreciating this simple Drucker maxim? For generations, management thinking and management education have rested on the intellectual framework and assumptions of three core disciplines: Mathematics (plus engineering), Economics and Psychology. Money and markets have been explained respectively by mathematics and economics, while human behaviour in business has been explained by psychology. These disciplines have served business well and have helped create the foundation of contemporary management practice.

This book outlines a new management paradigm, one wherein the disciplinary assumptions shift from the purely analytical and calculative disciplines of mathematics, economics and psychology, to the action-oriented, experienced-based disciplines of Design, Architecture and Anthropology. The hub of the wheel that connects design, architecture and anthropology is *innovation*. Anthropology (and ethnography) is the source of ever-deeper insights into the natural, sometimes unarticulated, desires and aspirations of consumers and employees. Architecture is a way of thinking that must relate contraints to the building of new things. Design is both a way of thinking about the world and a methodology for building new things. It transforms consumer insights into new products, experiences, business models and work processes.

The hub of the wheel that connects design, architecture and anthropology is *innovation*.

A view of the Mathematics/Economics/Psychology paradigm contrasted with the Architecture/Design/Anthropology paradigm looks like this:

M/E/P Model	A/D/A Model
'Managing the Known'	'Building the Unknown'
through:	through:
* Mathematics * Economics * Psychology	* Architecture * Design * Anthropology
for:	for:
* Replication & Scale	* Emergence/differentiation
learned in:	learned in:
* MBA programs	* MBD programs

This book outlines a shift from a traditional approach, 'managing the known', to a design and innovation approach, 'building the unknown'.

The emphasis in the A/D/A model falls more on building and doing and less on analytical abstractions such as planning, strategy and policy formation. The shift is from a traditional approach, 'managing the known', to a design and innovation approach, 'building the unknown'. As Herbert Simon argued in the 1960s, it is only our hubris that leads us to assume we have full and perfect information before we implement grand strategies. In practice, our rationality (and information) is bounded and we learn most effectively by doing, taking stock, iterating (doing again), taking stock, iterating and so forth. IDEO Chief Executive Tim Brown has referred to the fundamentals of the 'design as strategy' approach as a process of *building to think*, which seems to me to capture brilliantly the spirit of the design-driven approach to innovation.

1.6   The 'Design Revolution'

The shift from M/E/P to A/D/A does not just happen through words. It requires a certain worldview, a method and a methodology. This is where design thinking, as a way of viewing the world and a way of solving problems, is important. Roger Martin, Dean of the Rotman School of Management at the University of Toronto, has articulated more clearly than perhaps any other mainstream business voice the case for what he calls a 'design revolution' to take place in the world of business. Co-founder and former director of Monitor Group Consulting, Martin is not a career academic. When he left Monitor to return to his native Canada to lead the Rotman School, Martin was on a mission. He took a massive pay cut in making the transition into academia and since then Rotman has climbed to the top echelon in most global business school rankings. This has been due in large part to the way that Rotman has restructured its core offerings around the principles of design, innovation and integrative and interdisciplinary thinking. It has initiated collaborative curricula with the Ontario College of Art and Design, with whom it is building a new generation of management education, blending business with art and design. Commenting on Martin's work at Rotman, Peter Drucker once stated that: 'what the Rotman School is doing may be the most important thing happening in management education today'. What is this new thing? How does it impact upon management education, management practice and, most importantly, the practice of innovation?

Martin has written prolifically about what he sees as the design 'imperative' or 'design revolution' that is re-defining global competitive strategy today. He talks about this in terms of a paradigm shift or movement from a traditionalist view of the centralized firm to a design-focused, decentralized view of the firm:

'Value creation in the 20th century was about taking a fundamental understanding of a 'mystery' - a heuristic - and driving it to a formula, an algorithm - so that it could be driven to huge scale and scope.'

As we leave behind one economic age and enter another, many of our philosophical assumptions about what constituted competitive success grew out of a different world. Value creation in the 20th century was largely defined by the conversion of *heuristics* to *algorithms*. It was about taking a fundamental understanding of a 'mystery' - a heuristic - and driving it to a formula, an algorithm - so that it could be driven to huge scale and scope. As a result, many 20th century organizations succeeded by instituting fairly linear improvements, such as re-engineering, supply chain management, enhanced customer responsiveness, and cost controls. These ideas were consistent with the traditional Taylorist view of the company as a centrally-driven entity that creates wealth by getting better and better at doing the same thing.

McDonalds, Dell, EDS and Wal-Mart have all standardized to global scale via finely tuned algorithms of replication and sameness.

Examples of firms that have succeeded in a traditional way, according to Martin, are McDonalds, Dell, EDS and Wal-Mart, all of which have standardized to global scale via finely tuned algorithms of replication and sameness.

The Taylorist view of the firm cannot explain, though, the success of firms such as Apple, Google, BMW, Whole Foods, Starbucks, *Fast Company* magazine, the new P&G or Microsoft. These firms thrive on a combination of research, innovation, creativity and being systematic. They are better than the competition at generating new things and experiences for customers. Martin frames it in the following way, suggesting that:

> Competition is no longer in global scale intensive industries; rather, it's in non-traditional, imagination-intensive industries. Today's businesses are sensing an increased demand for speed in product development, design cycles, inventory turns, and competitive response, and there are major implications for the individuals within those organizations. I would argue that in the 21st century, value creation will be defined more by the conversion of *mysteries* to *heuristics* - and that as a result, we are on the cusp of a design revolution in business.

Underlying the shift towards design thinking is a generational and cultural shift wherein employees in their 30s and 40s now expect and demand working arrangements, styles and content that are more in line with Martin's thinking than they are with those of the traditionalist firm. Also, in light of the fact that millions of baby boomer senior corporate managers are set to retire in the next five years, the managerial implications of this shift become very real. This demographic reality poses significant and long-term challenges for the overall management of human resources in the global economy. In turn, the expectations of the new generation of managers will demand that companies become more innovative and will affect changes at an organizational level, from who is recruited to how people are managed. Martin presents the move from 'traditional' to 'design' in the following schematic:

FEATURE	FROM 'TRADITIONAL FIRM'	TO 'DESIGN SHOP'
Flow of Work Life	* Ongoing tasks * Permanent assignments	* Projects * Defined terms
Source of Status	* Managing big budgets and large staffs	* Solving 'wicked problems'
Style of Work	* Defined roles * Wait until it is 'right'	* Collaborative * Iterative
Mode of Thinking	* Deductive * Inductive	* Deductive * Inductive * 'Abductive'
Dominant Attitude	* We can only do what we have budget to do * Constraints are the enemy	* Nothing can't be done * Constraints increase the challenge and excitement

To attract and retain the types of Generation X and Generation Y employees who will drive tomorrow's innovative companies, a whole menu of new organizational commitments will become increasingly important.

To attract and retain the types of Generation X and Generation Y employees who will drive tomorrow's innovative companies (that is, those people who combine right-brain and left-brain skills and values), a whole menu of new organizational commitments will become increasingly important.

Bridging left-brain and right-brain, the *doing* with the *empathy*, is what IDEO's Tim Brown refers to when he discusses the importance of 'T-Shaped' people to IDEO's success:

> Regardless of whether your goal is to innovate around a product, service, or business opportunity, you get good insights by having an observant and empathetic view of the world. You can't just stand in your own shoes; you've got to be able to stand in the shoes of others. Empathy allows you to have original insights about the world. It also enables you to build better teams.

Brown continues, suggesting that the T-Shaped employee (or leader) is also a technically competent 'doer':

> We call them T-Shaped people. They have a principal skill that describes the vertical leg of the T - they're mechanical engineers or industrial designers. But they are so empathetic that they can branch out into other skills, such as anthropology, and do them as well. They are able to explore insights from many different perspectives and recognize patterns of behaviour that point to a universal human need.

T-Shaped people are able to explore insights from many different perspectives and recognize patterns of behaviour that point to a universal human need.

In some respects this book is concerned with enumerating those T-Shaped values, practices and *commitments* to employees and customers and to the way work is defined and managed. I see eight key commitments that re-state Martin's basic thesis:

1. Commitment to placing *customer experience* and *experience architecture* at the centre of the firm's work.

2. Commitment to *abductive thinking* and *innovation* where employees are encouraged to generate innovation opportunities for customers.

3. Commitment to *hands-off management*, defined by *interdisciplinary* team and *project* work.

4. Commitment to *work/life balance* being built into the fabric of the firm (note Google's 20% time, wherein employees spend one day a week working on one of their own innovation projects - more on this later).

5. Commitment to reframing organizational relationships with *constraints*, which become innovation opportunities and not deal killers.

6. Commitment to a new generation of leadership and management development grounded in *design education* as much as in business education.

7. Commitment to *employee* and *customer retention* in equal measure.

8. Commitment to the idea that business organizations can (and should) be instruments of *good in society*.

1.7   Outline of the Book

This book could be divided into three parts. First, in Chapters 2-4, I discuss the disciplines of *architecture*, *design* and *anthropology* as they relate to the new agenda for innovation. I provide examples of how these three disciplines are being incorporated into the daily practice of businesses. I also present the case of SAS Software as an example of a human-centred organizational architecture. This allows me to introduce the philosophy of architect Christopher Alexander, whose writings on the relationship between the built environment and the pattern languages of 'living organizations' and the 'timeless way of building' help me frame my overall argument. I try here briefly to introduce Alexander's philosophy of building to a general management audience.

Next, Chapters 5-10 present six case studies of innovative firms - Southwest Airlines, Whole Foods, Starbucks, Google, Innocent Drinks and Shanghai Tang - as the centrepiece of the book. These chapters provide the empirical demonstration of what successful innovation actually looks like.

Finally, Chapter 11 summarizes the lessons gleaned from the case studies and provides recommendations for 'Leveraging the Innovation Moment'. My conclusion outlines a design and innovation methodology meant to help those managers interested in making the transition, from 'traditional' to 'design', which Roger Martin and others are talking about.

2 Architecture and the 'Timeless Way of Building' at SAS

2.1 Christopher Alexander

Architecture is not just about materials and physical constraints - space, concrete, wood, steel, etc. - it is about the spaces that it produces and in which we live and work. It is such an elemental and everyday part of life that rarely do we pause to think how architecture frames and conditions our lived experience. In this sense, I think that architecture as a field and as a discipline is ripe with philosophical and cultural insight that can be helpful to professionals far removed from the field itself.

Architecture as a field and as a discipline is ripe with philosophical and cultural insight that can be helpful to professionals far removed from the field itself.

In particular, the architectural theories of Christopher Alexander, the British born architect who for years taught at the University of California, Berkeley, have been widely influential and have been incorporated and used by professionals in a variety of fields. Among computer scientists, for example, Alexander's ideas have been enthusiastically embraced for the vocabulary they provide for building database architectures, information architectures and use-case scenarios for navigating websites and intranet sites. Here I want to pluck Alexander's philosophy out of the context of computer science and drop it into the conversation among managers about innovation.

Nowhere in his writings does Alexander mention business, or even organizations, per se. As an architect, his interests are in building design, urban planning and design, architectural theory and architectural history. It is only by extrapolation that his ideas become relevant to the conversation about innovation. But I suggest that if we make that leap, the rewards from considering Alexander's work can be significant. He writes beautifully about the process of designing buildings and spaces congruent with human nature, human needs and aspirations and thus his work is a wellspring of inspiration with respect to developing the concept of the human-centred enterprise.

Alexander suggests that the built environment can potentially 'come to life' as an extension of nature if it is conceived of and executed according to what he calls the 'timeless way of building'. According to him, the process of designing and building houses, offices, communities or towns either *does* or *does not* resonate with the innate and organic qualities of human interaction. Similarly, the process of constructing buildings either does or does not align with and nourish the innate spatial needs and comfort levels of humans. This includes relationships such as where people sleep relative to where they work, play and cook, as well as issues of lighting and the integration of built environments into natural environments. Here I want to suggest that the health or ill health of a company, or any organization, can also be understood in relaton to human interaction and need. If, as some studies suggest, roughly 70 per cent of Americans dread going to work, what does this say about the way in which most of our organizations have been *built* and how little natural energy and self-motivation they are capable of drawing out of people? By contrast, companies whose DNA is defined by a 'hands-off, *thousand flowers blooming*' management philosophy are places where employees want to be and which have low employee turnover levels. Not insignificantly, these companies are often market-beaters in their industries - the one follows the other.

Simply put, some places are better places to be and in this way they also manage to get more out of their people. Alexander echoes this closely in terms of architectural design. 'The fact is that the difference between a good building and a bad building, between a good town and

> The process of designing and building houses, offices, communities or towns either *does* or *does not* resonate with the innate and organic qualities of human interaction.

> If roughly 70% of Americans dread going to work, what does this say about the way in which most of our organizations have been built and how little natural energy and self-motivation they are capable of drawing out of people?

a bad town, is an objective matter. It is the difference between health and sickness, wholeness and dividedness, self-maintenance and self-destruction. In a world which is healthy, whole, alive and self-maintaining, people themselves can be alive and self-creating.' If any one word could be used to describe the self-motivating and autonomous sense of energy that permeates the exemplar companies profiled later in this book, it is *alive*. These organizations are very much alive, in that employees want to be there, and they offer up the best of their energy and talent in return. The fact that employee turnover rates at these firms are at industry lows is proof that employees are engaged in this way and their financial success in the market place follows. Whether we use the term 'virtuous spiral' or 'human-centred enterprise' or Alexander's *timeless way of building* (organizations), I think we are talking about the same sorts of thing. Do our systems work with, or against, the impulses and needs of human nature? The significance of architectural and design thinking lies in taking seriously the challenge of *designing* and *building organizations* that are 'alive' in Alexander's sense. That this cannot be taken for granted is highlighted by the fact that so few of our business organizations manage to accomplish this 'life' in any meaningful way. It requires work and effort and that requires a commitment to building those sorts of organizations consciously.

The significance of architectural and design thinking lies in taking seriously the challenge of *designing* and *building organizations* that are 'alive' in Alexander's sense.

I recently gave a talk in London to a small group of middle managers from companies of varying sizes, from household name firms to smaller, private companies. I talked about innovation and about the challenge of building cultures of innovation, covering many of the examples I discuss here. The response, while generally positive, was something like this: 'Well, in those companies that might work, but it could never work in my company'. Few disagreed that encouraging innovation at the line level was a good thing, but there was a sense in which implementing such a perspective in their organizations would be near impossible. In a private conversation with one participant afterwards, she confided in me that in her firm there were so many rules and procedures that would have to be unravelled, and as a result so many people made redundant, that such a process of innovation-driven organizational change would never happen. As she spoke, I was reminded of other passages from Alexander's book:

> But as things are, we have so far beset ourselves
> with rules, and concepts, and ideas of what
> must be done to make a building or town
> alive, that we have become afraid of what will
> happen naturally, and convinced that we must
> work within a 'system' and with 'methods'
> since without them our surroundings will come
> tumbling down in chaos.

'We have become afraid of what will happen naturally, and convinced that we must work within a "system" and with "methods" since without them our surroundings will come tumbling down in chaos.'

2.2   Cultural Architecture and 'Human-Centred Management' at SAS

More so than in just about any company I am aware of, the principles, values and commitments of the human-centred enterprise are on display at SAS Institute, the North Carolina based software company. SAS (which stands for 'statistical analysis software') is a privately held company that builds enterprise intelligence software for large corporate, not-for-profit and government organizations. The company has around 6,500 employees and reports annual revenues of about US$2bn. Some argue that many of the employee-centric policies - and the resulting corporate culture - are possible only because it is a private firm and the owners are free to do as they, and not anonymous shareholders, want to do. The implicit critique here is that all the touchy-feely things that companies

At SAS the 'lavish' employee benefits not only keep employees happy, productive and loyal, they in fact save the company nearly US$85 m a year because of its industry-leading employee retention rates.

such as SAS do for their employees are too costly and are thus frivolous. However, at SAS the 'lavish' employee benefits not only keep employees happy, productive and loyal, but they in fact save the company nearly US$85m a year because of its industry-leading employee retention rates.

In short, the *cultural architecture* at SAS is rare, exemplary and highly effective. Jim Goodnight, company founder and principal shareholder, has very consciously and carefully designed a company that is profoundly human-centred. In the case of SAS, my incorporation of the architectural reference is only partially metaphorical. The built environment at SAS, and all that it includes, is very much a part of SAS's success. At many high tech firms, programmers are lined up in endless rows of cubicles, hacking out code with little or no sociality or comfort built into the work. Goodnight recalls interviewing for a job with a tech company years ago, in the 1960s. 'The programmers sat in desk after desk, lined up row after row, in a building that was like an aircraft hangar. No walls, no privacy... I hear that's what Cisco is like these days. And Intel.' Larnell Lennon, a software tester, came to SAS from Nortel in the early 1990s. Of Nortel, he says, 'The professional standards there were great. But you went into your cubicle in the morning, and then you left at the end of the day. The atmosphere was tight'. About this issue of work *context*, Goodnight says, quite simply, 'I believe a person's surroundings have a lot to do with how a person feels. We try to have nice surroundings here'. This is a classic Jim Goodnight understatement.

2.3 SAS's Human-Centred-Enterprise Commitments

There are several dimensions to SAS's Human-Centred-Enterprise Commitments: the company is family-focused; committed to employee wellness and encourages user-centred design and innovation.

There are several dimensions to SAS's HCE commitments. First, the company is extremely family-focused. Not in the platitude-like way adopted by some companies where they say that employees are treated like family, but rather, it is family-focused as it pertains to the employees' families and their work/life balance. The second dimension, related to the first, is the company's systemic commitment to employee wellness, both physical and emotional: the fitness staff and wellness coordinators are not seen as superfluous at the company. A third dimension relates to the environment for creativity, innovation and user-centricity that coexists with the company's deep commitment to its employees.

1. Family

SAS has become the world's largest privately owned software company while at the same time it has institutionalized employee programmes that many, if not most, employers would never dream of. For example, the campus has several on-site health clinics where employees and their children can see doctors and receive treatment, advice and medicines. Some 800 children (of 6,500 employees) attend either one of the on-campus day care facilities or its newly accredited kindergarten. There are private wings on several floors for breast-feeding mothers to feed their children through the day as they need to. The company's on-site day care facility is the largest in North Carolina and the cafeteria is supplied with baby seats and high chairs to encourage families to eat lunch together. Also, as a further emphasis on the importance of families, SAS has a seven-hour work day that is intended to push people out of the door by 5.00pm

David Russo, former head of HR at SAS, says that when the company was young and small, keeping its best employees was critical to maintaining momentum at the company.

'If you hire adults and treat them like adults, then they'll behave like adults.'

at the latest so that families can be home for dinner together.

A significant part of SAS's employee-centred philosophy has been focused on the particular needs of working women. David Russo, former head of HR at SAS, says that when the company was young and small, keeping its best employees was critical to maintaining momentum at the company: 'Our women employees were two to three years into their careers - at the top of their talent curve - and they started deciding to stay home and have kids. We knew and they knew that they'd have to start from scratch if they stepped out. Jim [Goodnight] said, "We can't lose those people. We're too small a company".' Thus began the company's day care, in the basement of the building it was in at the time. Extending from that, the company also encourages employees to do work from home when it fits their and their families' needs. The company allows unlimited sick days, as well as days for sick family and loved ones. If an employee is worried about an ageing parent who lives in another state, the company's elder care coordinator will help find a variety of care options to jump-start the process. As for sick days and being away from the office, Russo says: 'If you're out for six months, you'll get cards and flowers, and people will come to cook dinner for you. If you're out sick for six Mondays in a row, you'll get fired. [SAS] expects adult behaviour... If you hire adults and treat them like adults, then they'll behave like adults.'

One tangible result that has come about from the comprehensive commitment to families and particularly to women at SAS is that today around 50 per cent of the company's management is female: a rarity in the software industry. This goes back to the earliest days in the company's history when it first made its commitments to mothers, their families and their careers. From the perspective of organizational learning and knowledge management, the value of keeping product knowledge, process knowledge and customer relationships in-house is obvious. At a deeper level, though, SAS's human-centred agenda reverberates with Christopher Alexander's philosophy of architecture, space and the role it plays in the challenge of balancing work life and home life. This echoes his earlier observations on the way in which certain buildings, or in my discussion here, organizations, can be imbued with varying degrees of life and energy (which I talk about in more detail shortly). The possibility for a seamless connection between work and home is an ideal at SAS and the company tries as hard as possible to achieve this. Factoring out some of the more elegiac prose used by Alexander (which does not apply directly to the SAS case, obviously), his thinking nonetheless resonates with the SAS experience.

> For instance, in some towns, the patterns of relationships between workplaces and families help us come to life. Workshops mix with houses, children run around the places where the work is going on, the members of the family… may possibly eat lunch together, or eat lunch with the people who are working there…The fact that family and play are part of one continuous stream, helps nourish everyone.

Alexander's thinking is particularly helpful to the more specific experience of working women who have families and are as committed to them as stay-at-home mothers are:

> A woman wants to be a loving woman, sustaining to her children, and also to take part in the other business of the world; to have relationships with 'what is going on'. But, in a town where work and family are completely separate, she is forced to make another impossible choice. She either has to become a stereotyped 'housewife', or a stereotyped masculine 'working woman'. The possibility of both realizing her feminine nature, and also having a place in the world beyond her family, is all but lost to her.

Such choices do not have to be made at SAS, where commitment to helping families in the building of holistic and integrated lives is one of the cornerstones of the company's culture. One does not have to be a mother, or to have children, though, for SAS's human-centred policies to be helpful. The company's commitment to health, wellness and balance applies to everyone.

2. The Built Environment and Wellness

A second important dimension of the SAS way is its comprehensive commitment to health and wellness. This is another point in the employee experience at SAS where architecture, designed space and the built environment are committed in a distinctly human-centred direction. It is where architecture ceases to be a metaphor and becomes a daily reality in employees' lives. The SAS campus is massive and luxurious. In addition to its spacious and well-manicured lawns and gardens, the company's fitness facilities are generous and

Architecture ceases to be a metaphor and becomes a daily reality in employees' lives.

state of the art. It has 36,000 square feet of gym space, hardwood aerobics floors, two full-length basketball courts, a yoga studio, separate work-out areas for men and women, soccer fields and softball fields. It has a massage therapist on site and the company offers classes in golf, African dance and tai chi, among many others. Company health and wellness coordinators help employees with their specific health and fitness needs and routines and provide advice and assistance on an individual basis. So that employees can't make excuses for not exercising, the company has a laundry service that collects, washes and returns the workout clothes to employees' lockers every night. This way, the excuse of having sweaty and stinky clothes can't be used. Breaking from work for half an hour to take a yoga class, or meeting with a fitness coordinator during the day to discuss a change in workout routine, is not seen as a waste of time. They help create a healthy workplace. How could these things possibly be cost effective, a traditional manager might ask? How can something as airy-fairy as yoga contribute to the bottom line?

> How can something as airy-fairy as yoga contribute to the bottom line?

The return on investment (ROI) in the company's holistic management style and commitments, according to Russo and current head of HR, Jeff Chambers, is measurable. The company has an employee retention rate of around 97 per cent, which is one of the highest in the software industry. If you consider that replacing an employee costs one to two times the salary of the open job, the annual saving to the company of *not* having to refill those jobs is, according to Stanford's Jeffrey Pfeffer, around US$85m/year. As Russo said several years ago, 'That's the beauty of it. The cost of the buildings, of running the gym - that's

> Replacing an employee costs one to two times the salary of the open job; 'There's no way I could spend all the money we save'.

pretty inexpensive. There's no way I could spend all the money we save'. But at SAS, it is about more than just cost savings. It is also about more than being ranked among the 'Best 100 Places to Work' year after year. It is about building a unique institution that is meant, by design, to be balanced, holistic, sane *and* profitable. It is, as the University of Southern California's Ed Lawler would say, a 'virtuous spiral organization'. This is why business schools throughout the country write case studies about SAS as a new kind of 'balanced company'. However, despite the general recognition that the return on such human-centred investments, even on the very bottom line of the balance sheet, can be positive, many companies remain reluctant to commit in this direction.

In a recent *Business 2.0* article about how managers use excuses for not doing new things, things that are known to work and add value, Jeffrey Pfeffer begins with a cute yet illustrative phrasing of the dismissiveness he encounters when he writes about human capital for the magazine: 'Hey, Jeff. Love what you wrote about treating employees better to capture discretionary effort. Promoting learning by building a culture that tolerates mistakes? Great idea! Trouble is, we can't do it. Too much day-to-day stuff that takes precedence. Wish we had the time, money, and other resources to change the way we do things, but you know how it goes.' He continues expressing his frustration at the excuses and at what IDEO's Tom Kelley calls the ever-present naysayers in firms, suggesting that:

> It's as though a requirement for entering
> the ranks of corporate management today is
> the ability to generate excuses for why it's
> impossible to do things everyone agrees are

important. David Russo, chief people officer at Peopleclick and the former head of human resources at SAS Institute, told me that when he gives speeches about how to win employee loyalty, it rarely takes more than 20 minutes for someone to raise a hand and explain why whatever he is advocating can't be done.

Pfeffer's frustration is the same as my frustration. It does, after all, take courage to change the way we do things, even if (as we know) it can improve not only the experience of work but also the bottom line. There should be nothing coercive about advocating a particular type of change. What we can do is point out examples of companies, such as SAS, Google, Whole Foods, Southwest Airlines, Starbucks, AES, Semco, etc., that are financially very successful and competitive but that at the same time build humanistic management practices and conditions for employees.

3. User-Centred Design and Innovation at SAS

SAS has not become a leading global competitor in enterprise software simply by building gyms and holding yoga classes. The third and equally critical dimension of its unique cultural architecture is its customer-centred, user-centred evangelism. Implicitly, SAS understands the Drucker maxim of $I + M = V$ and it acts on it in a systemic way. SAS reaps huge amounts of discretionary effort from employees because of the goodwill, trust and loyalty that builds up over time. As one SAS employee puts it, 'You're given the freedom, the flexibility, and the resources to do your job. Because you're treated well, you treat the company

> It takes courage to change the way we do things, even if (as we know) it can improve not only the experience of work but also the bottom line.

> SAS reaps huge amounts of discretionary effort from employees because of the goodwill, trust and loyalty that builds up over time.

well… When you walk down the hall here, it's rare that you hear people talking about anything but work'. That intensity and focus drives the company to achieve about $2bn in annual sales.

Critical to the success of any programming-intensive work in the new economy is a combination of, on the one hand, technological wizardry within the employee ranks and, on the other, an outward customer- and user-centred focus. While the corporate market for enterprise intelligence software (how to find, structure, save and organize critical information across sprawling ERP networks) might not at first glance appear to call for 'creativity' as creativity is often conceived, actually managing today's star programmers and code jockeys can be a dodgy proposition. They know they are good at what they do and that very often their managers don't know what they really do or how to do it. They simply want to be freed up to get it done.

In their *Harvard Business Review* article, 'Managing for Creativity', Richard Florida and SAS's Jim Goodnight address this issue of managing creative people at SAS. They summarize the company's approach as following three basic principles:

1. *Creative people work for the love of a challenge.* For years we have known what motivation theorists have argued, that most people are more energized by work that is challenging, changing and stimulating than they are in boring and unchanging work that perhaps pays better.

2. *Recognize that creativity is everyone's business.* In a post-Balkanized company, the distinction between 'creatives' and

'suits' trivializes the work of both groups and yields less energy and productivity from the whole organization.

3. *Love your customers, they are the business.* SAS is aggressive and passionate about interacting with and drawing feedback from their customers. (They provide software for 96 of the top 100 of the Fortune Global 500 and 90 per cent of the top 500). Over the past 30 years the company has acted on 80 per cent of all customer requests for changes they have received.

On this last point, SAS as a company is something of a user-centred evangelist. It hosts (as other companies do) an annual users' conference, which Jeffrey Pfeffer describes as being very different from the traditional 'sales-pitch-in-disguise' event. Informal, low pressure, interactive and collaborative, Pfeffer has described the event as being more like a Grateful Dead show than a standard software industry event. The success of the conference illustrates that the internal cultural architecture at SAS is tangibly linked to its user base. SAS is human/user-centred, both internally and externally: customer experience and employee experience merge as two sides of a single coin, assuming different perspectives on the same architecture.

The internal cultural architecture at SAS is tangibly linked to its user base, and in this it is human/user-centred, both internally and externally.

2.4   Human-Centred 'Pattern Languages' at SAS

It might be helpful here to think of the organizational architecture and culture at SAS in terms of Christopher Alexander's philosophy of building. There are certain things - patterns, beliefs and practices - that most people in most circumstances connect with and respond to. Building an 'alive' organization almost necessarily entails including some (if not most) of the elements of an organic and sustainable pattern language. According to Alexander, the recurring behavioural patterns of a group of people - in a building, neighbourhood, community, town or city - make up the pattern languages of that place. As it relates to the study of organizations, I understand the concept of 'pattern languages' to be another way of referring both to the cultural behaviour of an organization *and* to the resource commitments that a company makes that sustain those behaviours. Some patterns that emerge from this consideration of architecture and culture at SAS include:

- Being involved in creating something new and exciting (i.e. not doing the same thing day after day, such as 'executing')

- Feelings of autonomy and independence

- Honest, trustworthy bosses and colleagues

- A balance between home life and work life

- Transparent and consistent pay structures

- The opportunity to learn and grow in a career

Borrowing Alexander's language and applying it to the cases discussed here, these are what can be called an organization's *life-giving* qualities: that is, aspects of work that are intrinsically satisfying and motivating for

SAS, and the firms discussed in Chapters 5-10 of the book, are rich in life-giving qualities: that is, aspects of work that are intrinsically satisfying and motivating for employees.

employees and a source of discretionary effort for the company. SAS, and the firms discussed in Chapters 5-10 of the book, are rich in these life-giving qualities.

3   Innovation by Design

3.1   What is Design?

Designers have never had it so good. Following years of being isolated in the studio, the lab or the gallery, designers now have the attention of mainstream managers and increasingly a seat at the table of corporate strategy. An instructive case in point is the French sporting goods manufacturer Decathlon, one of the Gold Medal winners at the 2006 Industrial Design Society of America awards competition. Decathlon received a gold medal for the 2-Second Quechua Tent, a tent that opens completely in two seconds after simply being thrown into the air. When it lands, the two-person tent is ready to go.

In April 2006, at the annual European International Design Management Conference in Amsterdam, Decathlon's Design Director, Philippe Picaud, spoke to an eagerly gathered crowd on the topic of 'Why Design is not an Added Value'. The private company, with 350 stores, 29,000 employees and an annual turnover of about €3.8bn, was a hot topic at the conference and Picaud's talk was well attended. Among other interesting questions posed to Picaud after the first part of his speech, were ones pertaining to the frequency and breadth of product innovation at Decathlon. Basically, the question was, 'How do you come up with so many breakthrough innovations so often?'. Picaud's response was simple, yet profound, as he tried to explain that design is not an added value (not more icing) on the cake of corporate strategy, but rather it *is* the corporate strategy: 'We build what customers say they want to use and how they want to use it'. More specifically, the formula for success has two essential design ingredients. First, designers and product developers are active users of the products they develop for customers. Scuba divers design diving gear;

The formula for Decathlon's success has two essential design ingredients: 1) designers and product developers are active users of the products they develop for customers and 2) the design studios are located inside its retail locations.

cyclists design bikes and bike gear; kayakers design boats and paddles, etc. Also, those specific design studios are located near the areas where they are most often used. Diving designers work near the coast; paddlers near rivers; skiers and cyclists near the mountains. Secondly, and equally important, Decathlon's design studios are located inside its retail locations, on the second floor of the buildings with an open floor plan and staircases connecting the sales floor and the designers' space. Customers are made aware of this and are encouraged to wander up to the designers to talk to them about their problems, needs and concerns. Designers walk down to the sales floor as well to ask customers questions about how they use certain pieces and how the user experience can be made better. Unlike many companies that claim, in press releases and public pronouncements, such things as 'serving our customers is our most important mission', Decathlon has turned this into an everyday discipline that drives the business itself.

But there is more to design than this. Design is more than just building clever products, though it is that. Design is a way of thinking, acting and, most importantly, *doing* in the world. It is about creating and building new things and experiences. And in terms of the bottom line, it is about growth through differentiation, innovation and sustainable competitive advantage. From IDEO's work with P&G and GE, to Design Continuum's work with BMW and Kitchen Aid, to Ziba's work with Lenovo and Umpqua Bank, yesterday's industrial design firms have become innovation consultancies that work at the highest levels of some of the biggest and strongest companies in the world. What are the larger lessons that managers and would-be leaders can learn from the current 'design moment' unfolding in American business thinking? What are the implications for the education, selection and development of future leaders who will be capable of

In terms of the bottom line, design is about growth through differentiation, innovation and sustainable competitive advantage.

directing 'differentiating innovation' over the long term? With design an emergent discipline in the managerial tool kit, what lessons do designers and the design community have for mainstream managers, leaders and for leadership education?

3.2   Elevating Design

The elevation of design as a key resource for innovation and strategy is tied directly to globalization. Emerging market economies are quickening the process by which technological innovations are being commoditized and driven towards competition-on price-only environments. The recent announcement by the Indian firm Infosys, for example, that it would no longer renew many of its call-centre contracts with Western companies suggests that Business Process Outsourcing (BPO) call centres have become too commoditized and unprofitable for some of India's biggest BPO firms. Their focus on winning higher value-added financial services contracts underscores this important trend within the global economy. In the context of intensive commoditization in both consumer products and business services, there has been a sharp rise in the premium placed on differentiation, innovation and the design of work that can subsequently be manufactured to scale in emerging market countries. Since Western firms can't compete with manufacturing operations in places such as India and China, their input into the global economy must move up the value chain, as Bruce Nussbaum argues. This has provided a significant opportunity for designers.

Design's marriage to innovation has emerged, in large part, out of necessity. Innovation and internal corporate growth are now top priorities and many companies simply aren't very good at innovation. 'Money Isn't Everything', a recent Booz Allen Hamilton study published in *Strategy*

> Emerging market economies are quickening the process by which technological innovations are being commoditized and driven towards competition-on price-only environments.

> Design's marriage to innovation has emerged, in large part, out of necessity.

The key distinguishing feature of companies that have high rates of return on innovation investment is often tactical and not purely financial.

& *Business*, shows that many firms that spend lavishly on innovation R&D have relatively little to show for it compared with some companies that approach innovation with much smaller budgets. The key distinguishing feature of companies that have high rates of return on innovation investment is often tactical and not purely financial. Yet, getting the innovation investment right is clearly an important corporate priority. A 2005 Boston Consulting Group/*Business Week* study of the 'World's Most Innovative Companies', provides some very interesting and useful data. Of the senior executives surveyed, 72 per cent said that innovation was a top-3 priority for the coming year and 940 of 1,000 top leaders said that 'increasing top-line revenue through innovation' had become critical to success in their industry. For example, at GE, which has embraced innovation and design thinking under Jeffrey Immelt's leadership, a goal has been set to increase internal, organic growth from about 5 per cent to 8 per cent in the coming decade. From an acquisition/operations/'Six Sigma'-oriented company under Jack Welch, to Immelt's current collaboration with P&G and IDEO on building a culture of innovation and risk taking, GE is in many respects a case study in the paradigm shift that is taking place in the design economy.

Generations of 'managerial common sense' have defined organizational structures, processes and assumptions to such a degree that the introduction of 'design thinking' into mainstream management is something of a 'revolution'.

However, innovation does not just happen by fiat. Decades, indeed generations, of 'managerial common sense' have defined organizational structures, strategic commitments, job descriptions, budgeting practices and industry-structure assumptions to such a degree that the introduction of 'design thinking' into mainstream management is, as Roger Martin has suggested, something of a 'revolution'. It entails some throwing out and starting over and this is never easy or readily accepted. To move from the M/E/P model and frame of reference to the A/D/A model is, admittedly, revolutionary in some respects, though it has been done and is being done via the disciplines of innovation I am talking about here. While *architecture*, as discussed in the previous chapter, is to a significant extent a source metaphor for the move from 'managing the known' to 'building the unknown', *design* and *ethnography* are hands-on practices and commitments that innovative companies are embracing today. Some of the largest and most established firms in the world, from GE to P&G to Credit Suisse to Bank of America (BoA), are embracing the design imperative. I'll look at some of these examples now.

3.3   Innovation at GE

Even at General Electric, getting 'out of the office' to better understand customer experience is becoming part of the company's culture. When asked recently about GE's new focus on innovation and organic growth, CEO Jeffrey Immelt replied: 'We need to be focused on where our customers are going. We should be playing into the major demographic trends and the needs of our customers... We're trying to stimulate new thinking by bringing people in from the outside, such as IDEO, to make sure we're not too internally focused.' Immelt reflects on these changes at GE and how they are transforming the core leadership skills that now drive the company's leadership training at its famous campus in Crotonville, New York. Leaders are now expected to have more domain expertise and industry specific knowledge; they are rewarded and promoted based on 'new business concepts' brought to light and to market and they are encouraged to engage actively in creativity-enhancing programmes at the company's partnership innovation lab, the GYM, which they share with P&G. Whereas in the Jack Welch era, aspiring managers who stayed for more than three years in a particular business were seen as failures, today they are encouraged, and incentivized, to get deeply into a

Today managers are encouraged, and incentivized, to get deeply into a particular industry and its customer experience and then to innovate for those experiences.

particular industry and its customer experience and then to innovate for those experiences.

Over the past couple of years, Immelt has committed $5bn to 80 projects that have come from his Imagination Breakthroughs challenge, where he has challenged top managers to generate viable new businesses to take to market. Now that their performance is being evaluated on these types of innovation-based criteria, many long-term GE employees are struggling. For example, '20 per cent of 2005 bonuses [were based on] meeting pre-established measures of how well a business is improving its ability to meet customer needs'. As the *Business Week* article continues, it describes the cultural shift at GE: 'Many of the company's 307,000 workers weren't exactly hired to be part of a diverse, fleet-footed army of visionaries who are acutely sensitive to customers' needs'. Or, as one outside consultant who has worked with GE on the cultural change puts it, 'These guys just aren't dreamer types… It almost seems painful to them, like a waste of time'.

3.4   P&G

The use of observational techniques and close interaction with customer experience as well as going shopping for one's own products (as a customer) is not just for marketing professionals any more. Leading companies such as Procter and Gamble and Credit Suisse are using these methods to develop their managers in such a way that personal development, customer intimacy and sustainable innovation become part of the same equation. At P&G, for example, Chief Executive A. G. Laffley last year gathered the members of P&G's Global Leadership Council of 40 business unit leaders in San Francisco, to work with IDEO to learn how to dive more deeply into understanding their customers' experiences across product

IDEO's first directive to the
P&G group: Go Shopping!

lines and geographies. IDEO's first directive to the P&G group: Go Shopping! The idea behind sending P&G's top leaders shopping was to force them to interact with customers, to see what they see and to try to produce some of the empathy for consumer experience and needs that IDEO's Tim Brown talks about. For IDEO the goal of this type of executive development is not meant to be mere fun or idle shopping. The goal is for individual participants to identify specific innovation opportunities for the company by seeing products, spaces and interactions from the customer's perspective.

A. G. Laffley's group was sent to buy music in three separate places: a small, funky music store, a large retail store and then online. Another group was sent to one of San Francisco's poorest neighbourhoods to shop for P&G products to try and develop a sense of how P&G's many customers in developing countries might see their products. Today much of P&G's growth is in emerging market economies, what C. K. Prahalad calls the 'fortune at the bottom of the pyramid' or 'innovation in the sandbox', and P&G is taking this demographic reality very seriously. The San Francisco shopping trip in the Mission District was in some respects an applied ethnographic outing.

Tim Brown says: 'any
real-world strategy starts
with having fresh, original
insights about your market
and your customers. Those
insights come only when
you observe directly what's
happening in your market'.

About the technique of physically interacting with the customer experience, Tim Brown says that 'any real-world strategy starts with having fresh, original insights about your market and your customers. Those insights come only when you observe directly what's happening in your market'. The commitment to getting closer to both articulated and unarticulated customer needs has paid off for P&G in the form of the world's first stand-up toothpaste dispenser made by Crest and the Swiffer mop designed by Design Continuum, which has made the company over $315m. The Mr Clean MagicReach retractable broom, which was developed as a result of watching several groups of women cleaning their homes in South America, has generated millions of dollars in revenues as well.

Of the CEOs of larger companies in the US, Laffley is one of the more enthusiastic proponents of design thinking and design methodology as central features of his strategy. A recent *Harvard Business Review* article, 'Connect and Develop: Inside Procter & Gamble's New Model for Innovation', outlines the ongoing process by which P&G is building an open-source innovation network. The network draws in expertise from outside the organization and drives its connection to research and knowledge from beyond its organizational borders. Like GE, but thus far much more comprehensively, P&G embodies the transformation from a traditional product-driven firm into a design-oriented consumer experience-focused firm: the type of transformation talked about by Roger Martin. The impact of design thinking has trickled down throughout P&G's culture, distilled into the three-part mantra that P&G-ers now espouse:

1. The customer is boss

2. The first moment of truth (how the consumer reacts to the product on the shelf)

3. The second moment of truth (how the customer reacts when actually using the product)

While P&G frequently uses other design firms to help with specific product developments, Laffley is outwardly very grateful for the work that IDEO has done for P&G in terms of shifting its thinking over the past several years. To repeat a phrase that Laffley uses often, he sees IDEO (and by extension other design firms) as 'a strategic partner' and not only as an industrial design shop. Importantly, this also underscores the shift that design firms have undergone, from being one-off product developers to being innovation consultancies prepared to take on large-scale organizational transformations as well.

3.5   Customer Immersion at Credit Suisse

Almost every company has something about customer focus in its mission statement. Trouble is, the larger the organization, the more executives tend to insulate themselves from customers. Some rely on customer satisfaction surveys and focus groups. Others simply assume that customers are just like them.

Fast Company Magazine

The danger of assuming that you know your customers is that you end up making products and experiences that suit yourself but not necessarily anyone else.

David McQuillen, customer experience evangelist at Credit Suisse, says that the danger of assuming that you know your customers (from traditional research methods such as questionnaires and focus groups) is that you end up making products and experiences that suit yourself but not necessarily anyone else. McQuillen suggests that to get around this insulation, 'You need to go out and talk to customers to find out what they want'.

McQuillen's approach at Credit Suisse has been to implement a programme of what he calls an 'experience immersion' exercise for Credit Suisse's top executives. The project entails visits to several branches of the bank, where the participants are asked to observe the process 'as a customer'. At the first branch, McQuillen teaches the participants to observe customers closely; at the second branch they are required to start and complete a typical customer transaction and at the third branch they are given a few questions to help start a conversation with a customer. The third task, according to McQuillen, is usually the most intimidating for Credit Suisse's

Often Credit Suisse's senior managers were so far removed from the experience of their customers that they appeared shaken by the challenge of being face to face with them.

senior managers. Often they are so far removed from the experience of their customers that they appear shaken by the challenge of being face to face with them, as if they are afraid of what they might learn. In a follow up session at McQuillen's office, the participating executives are required to navigate the bank's web site to check interest rates or the availability of a certain type of mortgage, or to see which of the company's bank cards could be used on a hypothetical trip overseas.

McQuillen suggests that the immersion programme has produced specific customer innovations, from reducing waiting time at a few branches to placing more useful signage in most of them. Credit Suisse's Chief Operating Officer, Christoph Bruner, said of the programme: 'In some cases, we actually made it hard for customers to do business with us. I saw that little things make a big difference... As a bank, we often think that only the financial products themselves matter - but there is so much more that goes on around that.' It is difficult to know what those other things are until you see them yourself, as Tim Brown often suggests. This is the very type of *external focus* that GE is currently prioritizing, as are P&G, Starbucks, Decathlon, Southwest Airlines and others. It only seems radical because it is not part of the traditional managerial view of the world. What I am talking about is not simply 'management by walking around', or periodically paying a visit to one's customers. Those sorts of activities have been going on for years, but not systematically and not necessarily very seriously. McQuillen quips about this, 'you can do this stuff in two or three days - you don't have to spend half a million dollars on research. Just go out and observe'. Often, as Tim Brown suggests and as the recent innovation study by Booz Allen Hamilton echoes, innovation is not necessarily expensive. It is an opportunistic frame of mind, born of

Innovation is not necessarily expensive. It is an opportunistic frame of mind, born of a certain view of the world and an understanding of a certain methodology.

a certain view of the world and an understanding of a certain methodology.

Traditionally left to the marketing and advertising departments, customer experience immersion needs to be extended to a firm's top management, across all departments and divisions. That is, if a firm is to act systematically on Drucker's maxim ($I + M = V$), then this must be the case. Hanging out in the back office, writing reports and giving orders, is empty activity if you do not know what is going on 'out there' with customers. Building in this type of customer experience immersion can help make innovation part of the leadership development process itself, as is the case at P&G and Credit Suisse. For innovation to become a cultural value across a firm, a company's top people must get out there, share the consumer experience and become credible to all involved constituents.

3.6   IDEO and Bank of America

BoA recently determined that there were untapped service innovation opportunities in its retail operations and turned to IDEO for help in finding something 'new'. Particularly, BoA believed that one poorly understood and under-served market segment - female baby boomers with children - was all but neglected in its corporate thinking. With very little movement or change in this demographic's relationship with the bank for many years, the goal of the BoA/IDEO initiative was to try to get this group to open new current/checking and savings accounts with the bank. BoA sent a group of IDEO ethnographers (which I talk about in greater detail in the next chapter) to bank branches in several markets to observe and interact with women in this segment and to interview them about their spending, saving and banking habits and tendencies. The markets chosen for the research were Atlanta, Baltimore and San Francisco. The ethnographers spent time with the mothers in their homes and hung out with them when they paid their bills and balanced their chequebooks. They also accompanied mothers on their daily routines as they dropped their children at school, went shopping and took their children to family restaurants. The in-depth ethnographic research with this group provided two very significant insights. First, many of the women in the study group regularly rounded up (for simplicity) when they recorded payments in their chequebooks or entered expenditures from ATMs and credit or debit cards. And secondly, many women with children in this age group expressed how difficult it was for them to *save* money.

Following two months of research, BoA and IDEO began prototyping by experimenting with possible solutions alongside real customers. An interdisciplinary team of financial experts, operations experts and consumer behaviour specialists held 20 brainstorming sessions with customers, generated 80 original concepts and boiled them down to 12 possible ideas. One of the concepts proposed 'rounding up the financial transactions of consumers and transferring the difference to a savings account'. One of the customers involved in the brainstorming suggested as a name for the idea, *Keep the Change*, which other participants seemed to like as well, and the name has stuck. As an incentive to get other customers and would-be customers to open new accounts, BoA agreed to match 100 per cent of the round-ups for the first three months after a new account was opened. Since Autumn 2005, when the scheme was rolled out, 2.5 million customers have signed up for *Keep the Change*, over 700,000 have opened new checking accounts and 1 million have opened new savings accounts. By any measure, *Keep the Change* has been a success and, like other initiatives launched by IDEO and their clients, it began in the consumer space and was built out collaboratively with customers involved the entire time.

3.7 'Business Design' Education and T-Shaped Recruits

While not as intense and dramatic as the talent wars that shook the business world in the late 1990s, there *is* a talent war under way in the corporate world today. This time around, the driver of the talent war is innovation. There are plenty of top line MBA programmes cranking out ever more graduates, but there is a growing premium on talent that it is capable of thinking in new ways and creating new things and new opportunities. An emerging generation of educational offerings, based in design thinking but focused on business, is beginning to fill this innovation void. Illinois Institute of Technology's Institute of Design in Chicago is one. The new d-school at Stanford is another. The Rotman School of Management at the University of Toronto is yet another. The Weatherhead School of Management at Case Western Reserve University in Cleveland has also begun to integrate design thinking into its core curriculum. And in Europe, the French business school INSEAD has partnered with the Pasadena College of Art and Design in Los Angeles to offer a 'concentration' in design and innovation.

Recently, *Business Week* provided a ranking of the top design schools in the world and it seems that the time has come when big companies are eagerly recruiting there: 'Looking for talent? Of course you are. A titanic talent search is under way as managers scour the globe for innovators. Companies are struggling to transform themselves from cultures driven by cost and quality control to organizations that profit from creative thinking.' This is not just at firms like IDEO and ZIBA any more. 'Corporations such as Nike, General Electric, McDonalds,

> There are plenty of top line MBA programmes cranking out ever more graduates, but there is a growing premium on talent that it is capable of thinking in new ways and creating new things and new opportunities.

Intel, and many others are looking beyond traditional sources of leadership to a new set of schools and programs to find innovative managers. And that's why Stanford's d-school has earned a place on our inaugural list of top d-schools'.

3.8   Stanford's d-school: The Hasso Plattner Institute of Design

In 2005 SAP Software's founder, Hasso Plattner, gave $35m to Stanford University to help build its vision for a state of the art Institute of Design. The school, founded and led by IDEO founder and chief engineer David Kelley, is in some ways a benchmark in the design education space. While there are other established schools and institutes teaching design to business people and business to designers, the Stanford school is symbolically potent in many obvious ways. For years many have referred to Stanford's Graduate School of Business as the 'B-school' (as it is one of the few top business schools in the US without a donor's name on the front door), now we will have to get used to talking about Stanford's d-school.

The d-school is an interdisciplinary place in its infancy. A graduate school only, it recruits designers, business people, architects, engineers, social scientists and artists to work on solving particular problems in teams. Precisely because it is a new school with its own charter, its curriculum and approach are intensely innovative. The education process at the school is a direct response to the call for making design education relevant to business. David Kelly says:

> At the d-School we're changing from a more conventional design school to a school that actually takes companies out there, takes students out there, and makes them follow

'[The students] need the visceral feel of the user experience rather than just sitting in their cubicle at their computer.'

somebody for a day and observe. They need the visceral feel of the user experience rather than just sitting in their cubicle at their computer... The big difference is the faculty and students come from different departments: business, humanities, engineering, so forth. We all work on projects together. In the past, group projects would be done by a group of designers or a group of engineers.

Now, though, with participants from a variety of fields involved throughout the process, the given problem or task is illuminated from all these different perspectives the entire time. This is central to the current success of the d-school programme.

The programme has been designed in an entirely new way: it is corporate-customer driven. For example, a sponsoring company that is encountering a problem, a real problem and not a case-study, will bring it to the school and ask a group of students to work on it. The programme is based on this concept of 'industrial sponsorship', where the learning triggers are the real issues of real companies facing real problems:

Companies want to understand our innovation process and put that in a mix with their process. They pick a project of interest to them. Nothing evolutionary like 'make the headlights open up faster on a car'. It's more like 'what's the future of the back seat of a car?' Or the future of gaming or radical cell-phone interfaces. So, Electronic Arts or Motorola sends a group of people to give us the problem, critique our work from time to time, and evaluates the outcome. From the company's side, you have 50 young brains working on the future of their product or service.

Reflecting on the developments so far at Stanford's d-school programme and the transformation of other d-schools towards a new type of business education, Kelley says: 'I think everybody's programs will start to change. Design is shifting towards design thinking and design methodology, which is really tied to innovation'. In this sense of bringing design education and business education together explicitly, the Institute of Design at the Illinois Institute of Technology (IIT) is at the forefront and their joint Industrial Design (ID)/MBA programme is of particular interest.

3.9   IIT Institute of Design

Under the leadership of Patrick Whitney, Director of the Design Institute at IIT, the joint ID/MBA programme at IIT has quickly become an industry leader. Whitney has consciously moved the programme away from a pure art-design type of school and has provided it with a clear business-education focus. In cooperation with IIT's Stuart Graduate School of Business, IIT offers a two and a half year programme that is both a Masters in Industrial Design and an MBA. Similar to Stanford's mandate discussed by Kelley, Whitney sees the user experience as the connector point between design (thinking and methodology) and business innovation. The reason that IIT's ID/MBA graduates are in such high demand, Whitney suggests, is because many of the firms that recruit there say they are facing an 'innovation gap'. Design, Whitney says, is perfectly positioned to fill the gap. But not, he continues, until design education itself is transformed into a more business-oriented form of education.

Many of the firms that recruit at IIT say they are facing an 'innovation gap'.

In the past, design education was focused on visual experiences, drawing and modelling. While many design schools still teach through largely visual methods, IIT has tried to be different. The ID curriculum is now focused squarely on the disciplines of business innovation and how they can drive corporate strategy. Most of the courses offered on the ID/MBA programme do not include the traditional ID activites that historically have been a feature of art and design schools. Core courses, for example, are:

- User Observation and Early Prototyping

- New Product Design

- Design Language

- Systems Design

Today about half of IIT's ID graduates enter corporate jobs in strategy, marketing, brand management and business planning.

Most of the courses interpret the design process in terms of solving specific business problems and today about half of IIT's ID graduates enter corporate jobs in strategy, marketing, brand management and business planning. While some design schools are consciously moving in the direction of business, innovative B-Schools like Rotman at Toronto (with Ontario College of Art and Design), INSEAD (with Pasadena College of Art and Design) and Weatherhead at Case (with Cleveland Institute of Art and Design) are partnering with art and design colleges to move their programmes in the direction of design. Weatherhead, for example, has engaged IDEO to design and co-present a course in innovation in its MBA programme, a similar partnership to one recently forged between NYU's Stern School of Business and Frog Design. The convergence of interests and teaching methods, it seems, can help both types of school take part in the interdisciplinary future that many management and design educators are talking about.

3.10 Rotman School of Management (University of Toronto)

Roger Martin, who I have talked about throughout the discussion, is, like Patrick Whitney at IIT and Fred Collopy and Richard Boland at Case Western Reserve University, passionate about design thinking and design methodology in the business context. In 2003, Rotman formed a partnership with the Ontario College of Art and Design to offer an elective course in design, design methodology, product development and innovation. Martin's goal for Rotman is to integrate design thinking into the core curriculum and eventually make it part of a new degree programme, something like a Masters in Business Design (or MBD). The ID/MBA programme at IIT is similar to Martin's vision of the MBD and Martin and Whitney work closely together in developing this new agenda for management education.

Martin's mantra regarding the need for design thinking is relevant here. He insists that a design-oriented style of management can move firms past the rut of sameness and scale, or the 'algorithms' that he talks about, by which firms 'keep getting better and better at doing the same thing'. The call for a fundamental transformation in the core assumptions of management education is becoming clearer and more consistent. I have referred to this earlier as a shift from a Mathematics/Economics/Psychology commitment to 'managing the known', to an Architecture/Design/Anthropology commitment to 'building the unknown'. It would be naïve to suggest that effective management education could exclude finance and accounting and I am not suggesting that. The issue, it seems to me, is this: in what basic framework and set of assumptions do the core courses in management (Finance and Accounting, Marketing, Operations, Sales,

In what basic framework and set of assumptions do the core courses in management sit?

Human Resource Management, Strategy, Management Information Systems, etc.) sit?

This remains an interesting and important question for management education. If business schools aspire to produce more graduates capable of contributing tangibly to companies that have an agenda for innovation and want to build cultures of innovation, they will do well to look on places such as Rotman, IIT, Weatherhead and Stanford's d-school. A new generation of 'T-Shaped' corporate leaders is being trained in these places right now!

4   Anthropology and Innovation

4.1   What is Ethnography?

As a subfield of design and consumer research, the anthropological research method of *ethnography* has found a new resonance within mainstream management. Long used by marketing and advertising professionals, ethnography as a partner with design on the observational side of understanding consumer experiences has now become a valuable point along the value chain of design-driven innovation. Sitting behind ethnography is a whole host of intellectual assumptions and frameworks derived from anthropology. As a holistic academic discipline, one that attempts to see the world across disciplines and silos, the anthropological perspective in business is, as it has been for a number of years, still in an early state of becoming. It is important to keep in mind here that since the late 1980s both anthropologists and journalists have talked enthusiastically about the potential contribution that anthropology can make to business and business thinking. Maybe anthropology's moment in the sun will only last for fifteen minutes but, as I discuss briefly in this chapter, those fifteen minutes now look rather promising. There are now teams of consumer ethnographers at some of the world's largest companies and many other companies outsource their ethnographic research needs to a growing list of ethnographic consultancies that are filling this market niche.

Whatever the longevity of anthropology in management turns out to be, there is little question that at present it is one of the ingredients, or 'disciplines', within the design-driven approach to innovation that Roger Martin, Patrick Whitney, Tim Brown, Bruce Nussbaum and others are talking about. Martin recently suggested, somewhat tentatively, that ethnography 'may become

Ethnography as a partner with design on the observational side of understanding consumer experiences has now become a valuable point along the value chain of design-driven innovation.

a core competency of the experience economy'. Bruce Nussbaum of *Business Week* is more bullish and outspoken in his claims for the significance of ethnography in the 'Design Age'. In a recent piece called 'Ethnography is the New Core Competence', he talks about the growing use of ethnography within large firms as a way to 'develop a deep understanding of how people live and work', as a way to peer into consumers' unarticulated and unmet needs and desires. Indeed, as I discuss throughout this chapter, Nussbaum has been one of the most enthusiastic champions of both ethnography and design over the past few years. In short, ethnographic research has become part of the landscape of innovation for many firms and associated consultancies.

Ethnographic research has become part of the landscape of innovation for many firms and associated consultancies.

Companies as different as Procter and Gamble, Marriott, Citigroup, Motorola, Apple, Starbucks, Whirlpool, Bank of America and Kimberly Clarke regularly outsource ethnographic research to a growing number of ethnographic consultancies. Also, some of America's most established companies, such as Microsoft and Intel, have in-house ethnographers who conduct consumer insight research for their companies on an ongoing basis. I will look at the Microsoft and Intel cases first.

4.2   Ethnography at Intel

It is not only pure consumer-oriented companies such as Starbucks (see Chapter 7) that have incorporated the ethnographic perspective as part of the work of innovation. Intel and Microsoft, for example, have in-house teams of ethnographic researchers that spend time directly with customers/end-users in their homes and offices to become better acquainted with how and why they use the technologies they use. Perhaps most importantly, they try to understand, by spending time with consumers as participant observers, what they will need and what they already appear to need but have not fully articulated to themselves yet. The Peoples and Practices Research Group within the Architecture Lab at Intel, for example, has anthropologists, psychologists and sociologists who spend time in people's homes throughout the world trying to understand the places/purposes of technology in naturally occurring contexts within people's lives.

Genevieve Bell, anthropologist and Senior Research Scientist in Intel's Peoples and Practices Group, describes ethnography as it is understood at Intel:

> Ethnography is a form of anthropological practice. It is both a methodology and a perspective. Through ethnography, we attempt to generate holistic accounts of cultures and peoples. At its core, ethnography relies on 'participant observation', i.e. the notion that you learn by doing and by watching, and by the interplay of those two roles. This means that anthropologists (and those from other disciplines who use ethnographic methods) do field work. They spend time in and with the cultures and peoples they are studying, engaging with the people around them, participating in every-day life, and attempting to make sense of the patterns of that culture.

At Intel, Microsoft and other firms that employ in-house ethnographers, cultural understanding is not a goal in and of itself. Rather, the idea is to connect ethnographic understanding to the development of new products and new service interactions. For example, in one Intel research project, the Peoples and Practices group interviewed individuals in 45 households from 5 countries in Western Europe with a goal of understanding unarticulated computing needs in households. The study revealed four 'domains of cultural significance' in

At Intel, Microsoft and other firms that employ in-house ethnographers, the idea is to connect ethnographic understanding to the development of new products and new service interactions.

Western Europe: 1) togetherness; 2) media experiences; 3) consumption patterns and 4) life outside the home.

What Intel's People and Practices team are engaged in more specifically is *design ethnography*, that is ethnography enacted primarily with the goal of designing something new for the specific group being studied:

Design ethnography is ethnography that is enacted primarily with the goal of designing something new for the specific group being studied.

> [The team] travels the globe to explore how people in different cultures live and work. In conducting their fieldwork, the team applies a variety of ethnographic and other social science and design research tools and techniques, from in-depth interviews, to story-boarding, participation in activities, and observations of people as they go about their daily routines… The work of the People and Practices team supplements and complements traditional market research techniques, such as surveys and focus groups. Such techniques can be used to identify trends and describe what people are doing, but not necessarily *why*. Social scientists and designers dig deeper, exploring people's values, aspirations, desires and motivations.

From the European study, *Looking Across the Atlantic*, as well as from similar ethnographic studies conducted by Intel in Asia, they have designed and built smaller and smaller processors for use in smaller PCs that require less space and processing power. What, for example, are the actual processing needs of a PC used in a rural village in India? This is the type of question that Intel is asking when it sends ethnographers to rural India. In response, it has built processors for small PCs that can run on a truck battery in conditions of extreme heat and humidity. In light of the potential size of the consumer market for technology in places like rural India, China and other parts of Asia, these sorts of ethnographically informed

In light of the potential size of the consumer market, these sorts of ethnographically informed design insights might become deep wells of business in the future.

design insights might become deep wells of business in the future.

4.3   Ethnography at Microsoft

A similar investment in ethnographic research capability has been made at Microsoft, where the User Experience Research Team (within the Windows Client Business Unit) employs a small team of ethnographers to spend time in the field with both individuals and small business owners. Microsoft is currently interested in deepening its understanding of the business computing habits and needs of small business owners and entrepreneurs, for whom it is trying to integrate and customize more effectively applications like Excel, Outlook and Word within its Office Small Business Administration (SBA) product. HP, Intel and Microsoft see a huge growth opportunity for technology products aimed at small businesses and Microsoft wants to connect with this demographic group's user experience in such a way that it can be the most responsive and trusted provider of their core business software applications.

Tracey Lovejoy, of the Microsoft User Experience Team, echoes the themes mentioned earlier by Intel's Genevieve Bell: 'The ultimate goal is to understand the holistic view of the world from other participants' eyes, as opposed to viewing the world from our own perspective. For Microsoft, this translates to understanding how our customers - and potential customers - experience the world and how technology fits into that experience... I try to help ground our planning and development in the real-world scenarios and behaviours of our customers.' Here Lovejoy touches on what other anthropologists in business, as well as people like Peter Drucker, say as a matter of fact: sustainable business is built when it is constructed by and for the customers themselves. This is precisely where anthropology as a discipline provides real added value to the business world. Tom Kelley, a general manager at IDEO (and younger brother of IDEO founder David Kelley), frames anthropology's contribution to the company's work in the following way: 'Far from being some fluffy, esoteric process of questionable value, the Anthropologist role is the single biggest source of innovation at IDEO. Like most of our client companies, we have lots of great problem solvers. But you have to know what problem to solve. And people filling the Anthropologist role can be extremely good at reframing a problem in a new way - informed by their insights from the field - so that the right solution can spark a breakthrough.'

'The Anthropologist role is the single biggest source of innovation at IDEO. Like most of our client companies, we have lots of great problem solvers. But you have to know which problem to solve.'

Specifically, the User Experience Group at Microsoft has contributed to the configuration of the latest iteration of Windows, where the team focused on issues around storage, metadata, communication and folder consistency. Several of the features in the current Windows application were directly informed by user needs as they were observed and later translated to the software developers back in Redmond, Washington. A larger and more ambitious project for the User Experience Group is currently underway in India, where members of the group are conducting fieldwork similar to that done previously by Intel. Researchers there are studying user needs at rural computing kiosks in remote villages, the information environment of micro-enterprises, household credit and decision making, featherweight computing and the relationships between computing and household well-being and socio-economic mobility. Some of these queries may appear to be far removed from the core software development work at Microsoft. However, as C. K. Prahalad and others have talked about for the past several years, the consumer market at the 'bottom of the pyramid' is not only in need of many things, but it also represents a huge business opportunity at the same time.

4.4   Ethnographic Praxis in Industry Conference (EPIC), 2005-2006

As an enthusiastic adopter of new consumer research methodologies such as ethnography, Microsoft recently co-hosted (with Intel) the first annual corporate ethnography conference - the Ethnographic Praxis in Industry Conference. In 2005 the conference was held at Microsoft's campus in Redmond, Washington and in 2006 the conference was hosted by Intel in Portland, Oregon. The stated objective of the first event was to provide a 'forum for ethnographic practitioners in business to exchange research, insights, methods and other information' with the goal of furthering the professionalization of the discipline within the business context. Ethnographers and other interested researchers from numerous companies have attended the event over the past two years: Pitney Bowes, Microsoft, Intel, General Motors, Yahoo, IDEO, PARC, Xerox and IBM.

Many of the firms that have enthusiastically embraced ethnography as part of their user research process are technology oriented. This in part confirms the critique that is often levelled at innovation advocates, who claim that all of this talk is perhaps relevant to firms heavily focused on R&D, but is less relevant for other firms in other industries. As the next section of this chapter demonstrates, though, firms from a wide variety of industries use ethnography to plumb the experiences and desires of consumers. Often, they turn to an ethnographic research consultancy to perform this research for them.

Firms from a wide variety of industries use ethnography to plumb the experiences and desires of consumers.

4.5   Ethnographic Consultancies

Key participants at EPIC over the past two years have been the growing number of independent ethnographic consultancies from all over the world that work on a project basis for some of the world's largest firms across many sectors of the economy. Here are just a few examples to give an idea of the breadth of application of ethnographic research in business. Ethnographic Research Inc., based in Kansas City, Missouri, has provided research services, videography, film and consumer insight services for Cargill, Dell, Electrolux, Kellogg's, Pfizer, Eli Lilly, Washington Mutual, Novartis, Tropicana and McNeil Nutritionals, among others. Ethnographic Insight of Seattle has recently completed jobs with Expedia, Banana Republic, 3M, Whirlpool, JC Penney, HP, IBM, Adobe and Harvard Business School Publishing. Ethnographic Solutions LLC of Atlanta has worked recently with J. Walter Thompson, Pizza Hut, Coca Cola and the New York Jets. These are small, private consultancies with very little available financial data. However, having tracked developments in this consulting space over the past several years, it is clear to me that the niche is still growing.

Nor is this an exhaustive list. Point Forward of Redwood City, California, for example, is an ethnographically-oriented design firm that has been integral to the development of several well known consumer products, such as Huggies Pull-Up Nappies, designed for Kimberly Clark, and the narrow Fridge Pack soft drink dispenser, designed for Alcoa. Both of these product innovations resulted from long-term field research, where Point Forward ethnographers spent months in the field with user groups for whom the clients wanted to innovate.

For traditionalist managers, these trends and developments in innovation research will likely fly well below the radar.

When most companies want to know what consumers want, they are likely to hold focus groups or administer surveys. However, as Genevieve Bell of Intel suggests, and as IDEO researchers also well know, what people say and what people do often have nothing in common. Seeing consumer behaviour in its natural environment, over a long period, can often beat the somewhat contrived results obtained by asking people direct and leading questions in a windowless room in a faceless office park in exchange for a handful of coupons.

> What people say and what people do often have nothing in common.

4.6   Peter Drucker, Consumer Anthropology and Innovation

At the beginning of the book I eagerly subscribed to Peter Drucker's maxim that the 'purpose of a business is to create a customer and innovate for that customer'. An extension of this maxim is my elaboration of Drucker's formula, which states that Innovation + Marketing = Value and that all else represents costs. If this is the case, then the issue of *truly understanding what customers are experiencing in their everyday lives* is of critical significance to business enterprise. It is for this basic reason that anthropology and ethnography have made their way into the innovator's toolkit.

I want to present a few final examples of how ethnographic insight can drive the design-led process of innovation. In 2004-2005 Sirius Satellite Radio hired ZIBA Design to dispatch a team of ethnographic researchers to shadow different groups of people from Nashville to Boston. Over a one-month period, researchers hung out with participants as they listened to music in various places, watched TV, downloaded music from different sources, read magazines, etc. What they found was that much of the media content these enthusiasts grazed on was stuff that they really would have preferred to store and enjoy later, not at the point of discovery. The result of the research was the Sirius S50, a thin device as small as a cigarette pack that can store up to 50 hours of digital music, video and commentary. It can also dock into a radio player and store satellite radio content for later listening. Simple as it sounds, nothing like it was yet available on the market (the S50 has significant additional capabilities compared to the iPod and many users rate it more highly). The device has already significantly increased the number of subscribers to Sirius. Of their work with ZIBA, James Meyer, Sirius President, says: 'Ziba's research capabilities and innovative approach to design concepts were most impressive'. This confirms what Tim Brown often says, that it is necessary to get out of the office, 'hit the streets' and observe real consumer behaviour in its natural context if you want to understand where the hot spots for innovation reside.

More recent, and more significant in terms of global impact, has been Ziba's work with PC manufacturer Lenovo. After acquiring the PC unit of IBM for $1.75bn in 2005, Lenovo has set out to design a new generation of personal computers targeted at different, culturally defined market segments in China. To help with this, Lenovo hired Ziba to conduct long-term ethnographic research among Chinese consumers to identify different types and categories of users. Ziba came up with four broad categories and helped Lenovo in the design process to target each group. Different computers with different aesthetic styles resulted from the engagement. For example, the Opti Desktop PC is a modular and configurable home computer that is designed to fit comfortably in the tight spaces of many Chinese homes and the Lenovo Evo Notebook/Toolkit PC is configurable as a laptop, a desktop computer, a TV or a digital music player. This sort of differentiated functionality within a single system is something that resonates in China more than in the US at the present time and it was something that Ziba/Lenovo discovered in the field.

ZIBA's CEO Sohrab Vossoughi understands the significance of the company's work with Lenovo, which speaks directly to the larger trends in the global economy and to China's growing significance within it, beyond just being a low-cost manufacturer. I discuss this in Chapter 10 when I talk about Shanghai Tang, the Chinese fashion designer that now sells a Chinese aesthetic in capital cities throughout the world.

> Lenovo had succeeded for years by manufacturing low-cost clones of Western machines while being protected by import/export laws... Lenovo knew it couldn't compete on price alone - its only chance was to out-innovate its competitors and create new products that had meaning for consumers. Lenovo had a lot of demographic information on its customers. However, in terms of attitudes, values and behaviours, Lenovo didn't know who these consumers were or how to develop products that would emotionally and functionally connect with them... They turned to us. They wanted to differentiate themselves from the pack and take a leap forward.

Here in a nutshell Vossoughi addresses many of the key drivers of a design-driven global economy: the need to move up the value chain from manufacturing to design, the related need for differentiation, as well as the research and disciplinary efforts that are required to build new things for customers - products that are culturally relevant and sustaining. For those firms interested in embracing innovation as part of their everyday work, the case studies presented in the following chapters will provide tangible examples of how 'defining of the new' and growth through

The case studies presented in the next section will provide tangible examples of how 'defining of the new' and growth through differentiation are already being achieved by industry-leading firms.

differentiation are already being achieved by industry-leading firms in different sectors in different countries.

5 Employees First: Cultural Innovation at Southwest Airlines

Not all innovation begins with the design-oriented approach advocated by IDEO, ZIBA and academics such as Patrick Whitney and Roger Martin. Obviously, many firms have been systematically innovating in various ways for generations. Southwest Airlines, one such firm based in Dallas, Texas, was in fact founded upon innovation and has consistently remained there for over thirty years.

5.1 Low Budget Airlines

Even the most revolutionary and disruptive innovations and technologies can be copied, surpassed, or routinized and commoditized.

Nothing lasts forever. Even the most revolutionary and disruptive innovations and technologies can be copied, surpassed, or routinized and commoditized. So it is no surprise that there are now numerous low-cost airlines that compete for market share with Southwest in the low frills, discount airline niche. In Europe, Easy Jet, Ryanair, Monarch, BMI Baby, Thomson and others have also taken a page out of Southwest's strategy book and replicated the model. In the US market, Jet Blue Airlines is a now a serious competitor with Southwest in this space and it is likely that there will be others in the future. However, Southwest is still the leader in the low-cost air travel niche and, from a financial perspective, it is the leader in the entire US airline industry. Indeed, in financial terms, it is the most consistently successful airline in the history of the US airline industry and it has achieved this bottom-line success by doing things fundamentally differently from the traditionalist model of management in the industry. It dared to be different, it had the courage to innovate and the results speak for themselves.

Southwest has been profitable every year since 1973, is the largest airline in the world measured by number of passengers and in terms of market capitalization is the largest US airline. No other American airline has been profitable for 5 consecutive years over the past 25 years, much less for 30 plus years straight. Shareholder returns for the last 30 years have been almost twice the returns of the S&P 500. In 2005, Southwest had a market capitalization larger than all of the other major American airlines combined. This basic financial information is presented as a way of suggesting that the human-centred corporate culture of which founding CEO Herb Kelleher is so proud is not simply a story of LUV (the company's stock symbol) and holding hands. It is a story about love and money.

A significant part of Southwest's success has been derived from the innovative point-to-point business model that the company has pursued since the early days, eschewing the hub-and-spoke model favoured by traditional airlines. The simplicity of the operational model at Southwest has enabled it to keep its costs down throughout its history. Add to this its connection to customers, through both its cheap fares and its comic in-flight customer/flight attendant experiences, and you have a winning formula. Southwest has flown in the face of convention since its inception. As a challenger to traditional managerial thinking and practice, Southwest is an exemplar of the type of company I am talking about here. While some managers and companies accept constraints as given, and simply subscribe to existing and known ways of doing business, innovators ask, abductively: 'How else can this be done?'. In the case of the airline business, the question would be: 'What other ways can an airline (without a ton of capital) come into being and legitimately compete?'. Using the language of design-led innovation here, the question could be framed: 'How can an unknown future of air travel be built?'. Meanwhile, traditional carriers continue today down the road to 'algorithmization' and

> A significant part of Southwest's success has been derived from the innovative point-to-point business model that the company has pursued since the early days, eschewing the hub-and-spoke model favoured by traditional airlines.

codification, in Roger Martin's terms, filing for Chapter 11 (bankruptcy) protection every six or seven years. Without the US government's largesse, particularly after 9/11, the situation in the airline industry would be even bleaker. So, while Southwest doesn't use the language of design per se, it has been consistently innovating in a human-centred manner for thirty years.

According to Herb Kelleher, the key to the company's success has always resided *inside* the company, in the way that the company loves its employees. As the company began to attract attention and scrutiny, especially after 1977 when it raised capital through its Initial Public Offering (IPO) on the New York Stock Exchange, investors, academics and analysts had questions.

'You put your employees first. If you truly treat your employees that way, your customers will come back, and that's what makes your shareholders happy.'

When I started out, business school professors liked to pose a conundrum: Which do you put first, your employees, your customers, or your shareholders? As if it were an unanswerable question. My answer was very easy: You put your employees first. If you truly treat your employees that way, your customers will come back, and that's what makes your shareholders happy. There is no constituency at war with any other constituency. Ultimately it's shareholder value that you are producing... We basically said to our people, there are three things that we're interested in. The lowest costs in the industry - that can't hurt you, having the lowest costs. The best customer service - that's a very important element of value. We said beyond that we're interested in intangibles - a spiritual infusion - because they are the hardest things for your competitors to replicate. The tangible things your competitors can go out and buy. They can't buy your spirit. So it's the most powerful thing of all.

'The tangible things your competitors can go out and buy. They can't buy your spirit. So it's the most powerful thing of all.'

Rarely will you find a business school professor, or for that matter a senior manager, talking about intangibles and a 'spiritual infusion' as being the differentiator that accounts for a company's success. But this is Southwest Airlines and this is the sort of language that they use.

Herb Kelleher says these things, people listen and many people confuse Kelleher with the company. Often, observers attribute far too great an importance to a company's founder, or current leader. In practice, while Kelleher has obviously been critical to the company's success, it has been the company's institutional policies and *commitments* to employees and customers that have made the difference. The philosophy of 'employees first' has been made real through policy commitments and practices that have established Southwest as one of the most human-centred firms in the world. As a result, it is no surprise that, like the SAS Institute, Southwest is ranked as one of the Best 100 Places to Work year after year.

In addition to the obvious business-model advantages and first-mover advantage enjoyed by Southwest as the first true low-cost carrier in the airline business, one of the company's great sources of competitive advantage, as Kelleher points out, is its idealism. Recall the earlier comments by Pfeffer, when he talks about the discretionary 'energy' available from employees who are engaged, well treated and happy. In this respect, the 'idealism' at Southwest produces a human-centred company that is highly productive (and profitable) at the same time. It does this in specific ways through specific programmes and practices and not in simple platitudes placed in the opening pages of the company's annual report.

5.2   Tangible Commitments, Not Platitudes

Since the company's inception, it has maintained a 'no lay-off' policy. With the exception of letting go individual employees for specific performance- or behaviour-related reasons, the company has remained true to its 'no lay-off' policy. Never was this more apparent and symbolically powerful than after the events of 9/11. While other airlines reduced staff counts by thousands, Southwest stuck to its long-held policy despite what this meant for them in terms of short-term revenues. When asked about what seemed to outsiders to be remarkable, one long-term employee replied: 'That's part of our culture. We've always said we'll do whatever we can do to take care of our people. So that's what we tried to do'. This is but one specific example of a systemic philosophy and commitment of respect for employees at Southwest. Author Jody Hoffer Gittell, in her book, *The Southwest Airlines Way*, refers to this as 'leading with credibility and care'. Former 'CEO Herb Kelleher and his top management team have excelled at growing the trust of managers in the field and frontline employees. They have built up trust over time by being up front and consistent in their message'. This translates into an authenticity and honesty at the company that employees are eager to talk about. One Southwest pilot said of Kelleher: 'When he talks to you, he is really focused on what you are saying. No one can pry him loose. I've seen this. He sets the example of respect for everyone. All are important. Treat each other with the same respect as our customers. So people are happy'. As anyone who has flown on Southwest airlines knows, its employees *are* happy, and silly and funny, and they actually make flying fun. In-flight crews as well as the gate crews are consistently upbeat, positive and unusually helpful - *and* the airline has one of the best safety records in the industry. None of this is accomplished by accident.

After the events of 9/11 Southwest stuck to its long-held 'no lay-off' policy despite what this meant for them in terms of short-term revenues.

5.3   Recruiting Happiness

Consistent with the 'spiritual infusion' that I alluded to earlier, Southwest places a high premium on *employees being themselves*. This may seem like a simplistic and obvious statement, but it is not necessarily the case at many traditional firms where conformity, gamesmanship and politicking are the norms. It is often the case that well-meaning and thoughtful people in many organizations must adopt manipulative and crafty workplace personas in order to navigate the backbiting and power plays. At Southwest, work/life balance is taken very seriously, starting with the assumption that people should simply be themselves wherever they are. As Kelleher says, 'We try to allow our people to be themselves and not have to surrender their personality when they arrive at Southwest'. One of their HR mottos is 'We hire for personality and train for skill'. That is, Southwest would rather hire an honest, agreeable and likeable person who can work collectively within a team than a star-studded MBA who can crunch massive numbers and produce beautiful financial pro forma reports.

In an article on the hiring and development practices at Southwest in *Fast Company*, Peter Carbonara distils the Southwest approach to managing human resources into four core principles:

- What you know changes, who you are doesn't.

- You can't find what you're not looking for.

- The best way to evaluate people is to watch them work (as opposed to relying solely on a battery of psychometric tests).

- You can't hire people who don't apply.

The connection between employee personalities and Southwest's employment brand is on the line every time a Southwest flight takes off. That people at Southwest like their jobs is evident in the attitudes they have as they interact with customers, so Southwest's *internal* policies of managing people and its *external* relations with customers merge into a single experience. Not all employees fit in at Southwest, or at any company, of course. In Southwest's holistic, collective way of working, solo-operators simply don't fit in. These people are quickly identified, given an opportunity to get on the bus and then asked to leave if they don't. This is not an anti-individuality stance. In terms of maintaining individuality and personality at the company, the focus is in fact stronger than at most companies. It is the employees' psychological security, in terms of maintaining their own unique personalities, that hopefully makes them more comfortable working in teams.

Southwest's internal policies of managing people and its external relations with customers merge into a single experience.

5.4   Empathy and Organizational Learning

From a knowledge management or organizational learning perspective, Southwest's 'holistic' and collective approach to work pays off, literally. Historically, most of Southwest's positions, as they become vacant, are filled internally. As a Southwest station manager explains: 'People move across departments a lot here. That helps break down status barriers between departments. It also helps people understand the whole process'. Nor is this approach to knowledge sharing random. The company operates a couple of specific job sharing/experience sharing programs that are grounded in the goal of building empathy and cross-departmental understanding. The company's focus on empathy as a central value in its management system is yet another thing that Southwest

The company's focus on empathy as a central value in its management system is yet another thing that Southwest shares with design-focused innovation.

shares with design-focused innovation, even though the company does not discuss its management style in these terms.

One of the programmes that the company ran in the 1990s was called 'Walk a Mile in My Shoes' and was based on participants spending a full day, or several days, actually doing the job of a colleague somewhere else in the company. Over a six-month period, 75 per cent of the company's employees participated in the programme. For example, Joe Dlouhy, a ramp supervisor in Orange County, California, 'walked a mile' in the shoes of Las Vegas ground crew member Randy Tagorda. In their book, *Nuts!: Southwest Airlines' Crazy Recipe for Business and Personal Success*, Kevin and Jackie Freiberg provide a long passage where Dlouhy discusses the experience:

> I reported to Group Support in LAS (Las Vegas) at approximately 11.30am, and started to work in Ground Equipment Mechanic Randy Tagorda's shoes. The soles of my shoes were worn out by 7.00pm. Some of the projects I completed included preparing a bag tug (mechanised luggage cart handle) for painting; removing a transmission from another bag tug; assisting in removing a transmission from a belt loader; and the finishing touch was painting a bag tug. Amazingly there were no paint runs!
>
> I never really imagined the hard work that our Ground Support team does. The appreciation to keep our equipment operational sometimes goes unnoticed. This experience helped me understand and take more pride in each piece of equipment that is used daily.

The company covered the costs of the employees who travelled to other locations to participate in the

Many companies talk about communication, openness, knowledge sharing and a 'one team' spirit, but relatively few companies actually commit resources to make those platitudes realities.

programme, so there was no cost for the employees. The programme provided a tangible and hands-on process by which employees from across different parts of the company could share experiences and come to understand the full breadth of work that goes on at the company on a daily basis. Many companies talk about communication, openness, knowledge sharing and a 'one team' spirit, but relatively few companies actually commit resources to make those platitudes realities.

The fulcrum of this 'learning across departments' and across disciplines is *empathy*. As the Freibergs say, 'empathy stimulates learning': 'It's amazing how much you can learn from simply putting yourself in another person's shoes. Southwest accelerates the learning process by encouraging people to understand other people's jobs. This stimulates cross-functional communication and reminds people that there are perspectives other than their own. Learning, sharing, and understanding are the result.' This perspective is straight out of Anthropology 101 and is reiterated by IDEO's Tim Brown when he says that putting oneself in another's shoes not only helps build empathy in a general sense but also provides insights into others' needs that can be an opportunity for innovating for those needs. Seeing work and life through other people's eyes is a key ingredient, indeed a cornerstone, of the human-centred enterprise. In this respect, the HCE, as I am describing it, could also be defined as an 'anthropological enterprise'.

Seeing work and life through other people's eyes is a key ingredient, indeed a cornerstone, of the human-centred enterprise.

A second empathy-generating programme that Southwest has used is called 'A Day in the Field'. Unlike the Walk a Mile programme, which was a one-off, A Day in the Field is ongoing and runs throughout the year, but the basic idea is similar. If one wants to spend a day or a few days 'in the field', then that is built into the schedule (if possible) and the cross-experience is made possible. Again, this is anthropological in that *understanding* and *empathy* are produced in the naturally occurring context of action and not in the office or in focus groups, surveys or other conventional methods of information gathering. Design methodology, as I have been discussing here, starts with this type of *in context* observation and witnessing of real behaviour in its natural setting. A Day in the Field is particularly powerful when someone from a corporate position spends a few days with front-line employees, whether a member of ground crew, flight crew or gate crew.

5.5   Great Service Begins at Home

With the intense focus on consumer experience and innovation that lies at the heart of my argument here, it might seem counterintuitive to say, as Herb Kelleher has, that employees should always come first among a company's main stakeholders. But this is not the case at Southwest. Southwest is intensely customer focused and has exceptional customer service precisely *because* it systematically treats its employees so well. It is what Kevin and Jackie Freiberg mean when they say of Southwest that 'great customer service begins at home'. Management guru Tom Peters interprets Kelleher's philosophy this way. While Southwest Airlines CEO Herb Kelleher gives customers a terrific deal on an airline seat, he makes it clear that his employees come first - even if it means dismissing customers. But aren't customers always right? "'No, they are not", Kelleher snaps. "And I think that's one of the biggest betrayals of employees a boss can possibly commit. The customer is frequently wrong. We don't carry those sorts of customers. We write to them and say, *fly somebody else. Don't abuse our people.*'" How does this philosophy work in action?

A simple example might help illustrate how Southwest's 'employee first' mantra can simultaneously be a customer-

Southwest is intensely customer focused and has exceptional customer service precisely *because* it systematically treats its employees so well.

centric philosophy. In 1994 one of Southwest's rivals offered up a computerized reservation system that travel agents quickly adopted. Kelleher was furious when the agents wanted Southwest effectively to pay one of their rivals each time someone made a reservation on Southwest through the system. He refused to use the new ticketing system.

Unbeknownst to him and the board, a group of employees from several departments - Ground Operations, Reservations, Customer Relations, Finance and Systems - had been collaborating to produce an alternative automated ticketing system that Southwest could use instead of the one being forced on them. The group didn't ask anyone for permission and felt free to try to innovate and possibly to fail. Without being directed to innovate with this solution, they were aware enough of the competitive external environment to know the threat. They also knew that Southwest's officers were serious when they regularly answered tough questions with, 'I don't know, what do you think?'. The Freibergs put it this way: 'When the systems, structures, policies, procedures and practices of an organization are designed and lived out so that employees genuinely feel that they come first, trust is the result. Southwest employees trust the company, and love its leadership, so they are not sceptical or apprehensive when management says: "Do whatever you think is right!".' In the case of innovating for automated ticketing, the interdisciplinary group that came through for the company knew, even as they spent a considerable amount of the company's time and money, that they would not be punished if they failed to come up with a viable solution. This sort of 'walking the talk' of employee-led innovation is rare.

> The interdisciplinary group knew, even as they spent a considerable amount of the company's time and money, that they would not be punished if they failed to come up with a viable solution.

Kelleher reflects on this values-commitment at Southwest as it relates to the example of their homemade automated ticketing system.

We're not looking for blind obedience. We're looking for people who on their own want to be doing what they're doing because they consider it to be a worthy objective. I have always believed that the best leader is the best server. And if you're a servant, by definition, you're not controlling. In an organization like ours, you're also likely to be a step behind employees. The fact that I cannot possibly know everything that goes on in our operation - and don't pretend to - is a source of competitive advantage. The freedom, informality, and interplay that people enjoy allows them to act in the best interests of the company.

In the reservation-ticketing example, the winner was in fact the customer. Southwest's automated reservation system, which now is driven primarily through its web site, drives down the costs of booking seats and has helped them keep their prices below those of their rivals. The percentage of online reservation bookings at Southwest continues to be well above that of the traditional carriers (and therefore the costs of booking are kept lower) and this particular employee-led innovation has contributed to this lead.

In a broader sense Southwest has been the most significant innovator in the history of the airline business, effectively defining the low-cost air travel market that is now a global business. Content to fly only domestic flights, Southwest now carries more domestic passengers than any other airline. It also has, as I mentioned earlier, a larger market capitalization and higher margins than any other airline, despite working with smaller operating revenues than some. Its point-to-point business model, driven by the quickest turnaround times in the business, as well as one of the best safety records in the business, make it the envy of the entire industry. The countless small innovations

Countless small innovations and process improvements, from both management and frontline employees, combine like *a thousand flowers blooming* to give the company a continuing edge on its competitors.

and process improvements, from both management and frontline employees, combine like *a thousand flowers blooming* to give the company a continuing edge on its competitors.

Despite all of this, the company's share price continues to hover below $20/share and traditional airlines are beginning to squeeze better margins from their traditional hub and spoke systems. Legacy carriers have been able to crawl back to competitiveness in the large part by mimicking many of the practices pioneered by Southwest. For example, rival airlines now offer more point-to-point flights than they used to and they offer prices that are now competitive with Southwest's. At the same time, Southwest's share price has suffered, in part as a sector-wide malaise hangs over the industry. But one thing is unlikely to change. Southwest will continue to be a great place to work, driven by a consistent and comprehensive employee-first set of policies. In the words of a Southwest operations agent, commenting on the accessibility of Herb Kelleher (before he retired as CEO and became Chairman only): 'If I didn't work at Southwest, I would not work in this industry. At the other carriers, they don't trust their managers. I have friends who work for other carriers and the whole attitude is just completely different. The CEO says something, and they don't believe what he says. Herb is so obtainable'. And, to the extent that systemic and sustained innovation most fruitfully occurs at the front line, at the employee-customer interface, Southwest's tradition and capacity for innovation is fully institutionalized. That, in turn, is a highly adaptive capacity.

5.6   The Pattern Languages of Southwest Airlines

Market success, innovation and adaptability at Southwest have not happened accidentally or incidentally.

Market success, innovation and adaptability at Southwest have not happened accidentally or incidentally. They are the result of consciously designed and implemented pattern languages of *value-commitments*, programmes, policies and practices in which the company believes and to which its employees adhere. Southwest has one of the lowest employee turnover rates in the airline industry *and* it aggressively compensates its employees with stock options. Southwest has evolved as close to Lawler's 'virtuous spiral organization' as any in the airline industry: this is a company that does extremely well in its marketplace while at the same time being committed to its employees and their well-being. One way to look at the 'pattern languages' of routines and commitments at Southwest is to extend Christopher Alexander's vocabulary to talk about the 'degree of life' that exists and thrives at Southwest as a social organization. That 'degree of life' is palpable when you fly Southwest, where you might see a pilot off-loading bags, or working at the reservation desk, or when a flight attendant presents the safety information like a stand-up comedian. As Dennis Bakke, formerly CEO at AES Corp., says, if work is not fun, it is not worth doing. Clearly, at Southwest, work is fun! Or as the Freibergs say in their book, it is Nuts!

As Christopher Alexander says, 'degree of life' is not meant in the biological sense, but rather in the social and structural sense. 'It includes the ordinary life, the actions and events which make us feel alive there, and which allow a happy everyday life to exist for the people... who live there.' The pattern languages at Southwest are not rocket science:

• Encourage people to be themselves.

- Give people the freedom and responsibility to make decisions that affect their work.

- Make senior management accessible.

- Respect their home life and allow employees to make that their top priority.

- Provide ways for people to job share to understand work and experience across the company.

- Let customer-centricity be a function of an employee-first culture.

- Employee-led customer innovation *is* the business.

- If the work is not fun, it is not worth doing.

As the Southwest case shows, when you allow these things, the customer is the winner in the end, followed by those who choose to hold the stock. This human-centred approach to management, or what Jody Gittell refers to as a 'relationship-oriented' corporate culture, seems like common sense to me, particularly in light of how well it works.

In an industry where very few companies are able to make a profit consistently, Southwest's success deserves attention. Its financial success, while it results from a combination of strategy, cost containment, fuel hedging, point-to-point travel and simplicity in its fleet structure, is also in part a story of how it treats its employees and customers and what it gets back from its employees as a result. Thinking of the 'discretionary effort' that Jeffrey Pfeffer mentioned earlier, Southwest clearly receives more than any of its peers. As Jim Collins says, 'If your competitive scorecard is money, you will always lose'. Suffering through the post-9/11 industry downturn did not

Southwest is one of the few HCEs in the airline industry (if not the only one), which is not unrelated to the fact that it is also the most consistently profitable airline.

drive Southwest to change its 'radical' no lay-off policy, something that clearly cost the company money. Much deeper than a purely technocratic 'balanced scorecard' metric, Southwest's metrics are both financial and humanistic. The 'degree of life' that it has engendered over the years, through systemic and consistent investments in its people and its values, is a significant hedge and risk management strategy that has a decidedly 'humanistic' quality to it. That is, Southwest is one of the few HCEs in the airline industry (if not the only one), which is not unrelated to the fact that it is also the most consistently profitable airline in the history of the industry.

6 'It's All Teams at Whole Foods'

6.1 Creator and Driver

Whole Foods has become an aspirational brand, at the forefront of innovating for the lifestyle-exploration and identity-expanding industry that now surrounds 'food' in all its dimensions.

Like Southwest in the airline business, Whole Foods Market Inc. of Austin, Texas has been a creator and driver of the upscale, organic grocery market business in the US and UK. Whole Foods has become an aspirational brand destination, a central location in the landscape of upmarket identity construction among mid-to-late baby boomers. Whole Foods represents an ideal - replete with dreams of organic, sustainable and ecological sourcing, multi-ethnic cuisines, 'foodie' and gourmet cooking styles and recipes and increasing sophistication in terms of wine and beer appreciation. Easily parodied by David Brooks's *Bobos in Paradise*, Whole Foods has nonetheless been at the forefront of innovating for the lifestyle-exploration and identity-expanding industry that now surrounds 'food' in all its dimensions.

The financial performance of Whole Foods since its founding in 1978 speaks for itself. In January 2006 the company became an S&P 500 company, reporting gross revenue of $5.4bn, gross profit of $1.65bn, gross earnings (EBITDA) of $431.7m and net profit of $173m. With a current market capitalization of almost $10bn, the once upon a time 'health food store' in Austin is now a global brand on an explosive growth trajectory. Indeed, some analysts have suggested that Whole Foods is growing too fast and that this represents a problem for the company. It operates 190 stores in the US, Canada and the UK and opens new ones regularly. The newer stores can be more than 50,000 square feet (4,500 square metres) and tend to be located in posh suburbs or trendy, gentrified urban areas. Combined, these factors make each store expensive to open and operate. Questions, such as how to determine how many stores are enough and how to grow same-store sales more effectively, are on the agenda. Yet the company currently outperforms its peers, registering 35 per cent gross margins last year, compared to 29 per cent for mainstream grocery chains as a whole. How Whole Foods has achieved this robust financial health is the most interesting part of the story.

6.2   Innovation, Creativity and Theatre at Whole Foods

At its core, Whole Foods is a 'lifestyle innovator'. The company has been innovative on three different fronts:

- Externally in the marketplace of the 'experience economy'

- Internally in terms of its team-oriented approach to personnel management

- In society at large as a spokesperson for new forms of sustainable, 'win-win' capitalism.

First, Whole Foods has been at the forefront of the 'foodie revolution' that has taken place in Britain and the US over the past two decades. Consumers today demand fresh produce and meats and care about such things as sourcing and impact on the environment. The range of products that a generation ago was available only at local health food stores has grown exponentially and many of these are now for sale at grocery store-size 'natural markets', such as Whole Foods, Trader Joes and Wild Oats. The stores are key stopovers in the experience economy and locales where consumers can announce to the world and to themselves who they are, what they value and which causes they support. That Whole Foods is an upmarket brand experience only deepens the commitment of consumers, who feel privileged, rarefied

The stores are key stopovers in the experience economy and locales where consumers can announce to the world and to themselves who they are, what they value, and which causes they support.

and ethically responsible when they support organic, fair trade agricultural methods and products.

If there is any truth to the notion that *you are what you eat,* then for millions of people Whole Foods is one of the key places within the consumer-culture landscape that facilitates the foodie revolution. This is particularly true of Whole Foods' new flagship store in Austin near the company's headquarters. At 80,000 square feet, it is a rare blend of Wal-Mart, health food store and grand theatre. The company is about more than just food; it is about turning something mundane - shopping for food - into something fun and aspirational. John Mackey describes this in the following way: 'Americans love to eat. Americans love to shop. But we don't like to shop for food. It's a chore, like doing the laundry… Whole Foods thinks shopping should be fun. With [the flagship store in Austin] we're pioneering a new lifestyle that synthesizes health and pleasure. We don't see a contradiction.' In a *USA Today* article about Whole Foods, Bruce Horowitz refers to the new store as: 'a better-for-you food bazaar on organic steroids. Or the grocery equivalent of Disney World for food junkies'. It is important to emphasize the 'health food' dimension to the Whole Foods story. At its core, this is what the experience at Whole Foods is about. It is about aspiring to a healthier, more balanced and sustainable lifestyle. As critics are quick to point out, Whole Foods is *very* expensive. For this, it has earned the nickname 'Whole Pay Check' among fans and critics alike. The expense, though, is part of the story itself. Whole Foods' executives believe that the ideas exhibited in the stores, which are divided up into food-focused lands à la Disney, could have the kind of industry-shaking impact on grocery shopping that Starbucks has had on coffee drinking. Whole Foods could help transform grocery shopping into interactive theatre. The association with 'theatre' may be a stretch, but the metaphor of a stage isn't that far off. Simply walk into one of the company's larger stores and, like flying with Southwest Airlines, the experience jumps out at you. There is a difference, and differentiation, in the value proposition of innovative offerings of all kinds and Whole Foods is no exception. From a purely strategic perspective, Whole Foods' cutting edge has been its ability to scale its deep differentiation relative to virtually all competitors in the grocery business.

Whole Foods' cutting edge has been its ability to scale its deep differentiation relative to virtually all competitors in the grocery business.

6.3 Growing Up

In its early days, the company grew randomly through acquisitions, with a sprinkling of optimism and passion. Today, while the passion is still there, Whole Foods does everything very consciously, even 'by design'. Their stores are, if not actual theatre, places for the imagination. Signage is never plastic but eco-friendly, made of wood-like products derived from wheat straw. The lighting is the same kind as that used in art galleries. The music is classical and soothing, designed to enhance the holistic experience that the products are meant to represent. The layout of the products in the store, as well, is carefully mapped. The 'experience map' of the consumer journey through a store is designed in a very particular way. Critics call it calculated and even manipulative and one psychologist suggests that 'Whole Foods offers a psychological absolution of our excesses. After filling your cart with sinful wine, beer, cheese and breads, you rationalized it's healthy, so that cancels out the negatives'. Yet, while the average supermarket records sales of about $400 per square foot per year, Whole Foods averages above $800. And, while average supermarket growth was about 1 per cent last year, Whole Foods grew by almost 15 per cent. Their goal is to be a $10bn business in 2010, up from $4bn in 2004. These are big numbers for a company that is often written off as a 'hippy business'.

Creativity does not come out of thin air. It is born out of the culture of the company, from the unique team-centric experiment in democratic management and democratic capitalism that underlies everything at Whole Foods.

What ultimately differentiates Whole Foods from its competitors is *creativity*. Most new stores are now Wi-Fi hot spots with sit-down eateries spread about in various locations throughout the stores. Also, more and more space in stores is being devoted to the high margin prepared foods items that other grocery stores now rely on. One industry analyst recently put it very bluntly: 'Traditional supermarkets don't have a driver to get customers in… Whole Foods has one thing that's lacking in the food retail business: creativity'. But creativity does not come out of thin air. It is born out of the culture of the company, from the unique team-centric experiment in democratic management and democratic capitalism that underlies everything at Whole Foods.

6.4 'Whole Foods is All Teams'

In addition to its market-focused innovation for Bobos (bourgeois bohemians) and beyond, Whole Foods is intensely innovative in terms of its core managerial style and approach. Its fundamental human resource practices mirror its overall human-centred approach to running the business. Like Southwest Airlines, it is an exemplary HCE. The company has evolved a unique and distinct culture, often derided by its critics as a cult, which in fact lies at the heart of the Whole Foods story. Similar to the virtuous spiral at Southwest Airlines, at Whole Foods the employee-consumer interface is the day-to-day defining ingredient of the company's culture. Therefore the temperament, personality and 'degree of life' embodied in the staff is the customer service that John Mackey sees as the driver of the company's success. In the holistic perspective of an HCE, the way that employees are respected becomes the foundation of the 'experience' that is delivered to customers. And since Whole Foods is an aspirational brand, this employee-consumer experience relationship is particularly important.

Since Whole Foods is an aspirational brand, this employee-consumer-experience relationship is particularly important.

At the centre of the customer experience at Whole Foods are the company's employees. This is consistent with Lawler's notion of the virtuous spiral company, where an idealistic and employee-centric internal management philosophy becomes the driver of external interactions (i.e. sales) in the company's stores. Former Whole Foods President, Chris Hitt, puts it this way: 'Customers experience the food and the space, but what they really experience is the work culture. The true hidden secret of the company is the work culture. That's what delivers the stores to the customers'. What does this mean? How does this play out in practice? How does Whole Foods build such a strong customer-centric corporate culture?

The principal building blocks of the organization are the 8 to 10 teams that make up each individual store. As he discusses in an early *Fast Company* article, 'Whole Foods is all Teams', Charles Fishman says: 'The Whole Foods culture is premised on decentralized teamwork. *The team*, not the hierarchy, is the defining unit of activity'. Teams are formed around departments such as produce, grocery, prepared foods, wine and beer, cheese, supplements, health and beauty products, etc. *Team leaders* in each store constitute the *store team*, store team leaders constitute *regional teams* and regional team leaders constitute a *national team*. Individual teams have an unusual degree of independence and autonomy. For example, teams decide if a new employee (a 'team member') is needed, then the team interviews *and* hires the new employee to join the team. New recruits are given a four-week trial period of employment, after which time the team votes to decide whether he/she is invited to join them full time.

'The Whole Foods culture is premised on decentralized teamwork. *The team*, not the hierarchy, is the defining unit of activity.'

Teams within stores compete with each other on established performance metrics and bonuses are tied to team performance. This functions as a disincentive for employees to hire friends who might not be productive employees. A slack new hire as a team member might mean less money in bonuses for the whole team. Bringing on new team members is not just about choosing someone who is likeable; it is also about choosing someone who is hardworking and productive. Recall Jim Collins' Premise No. 5, when he says that 'performance is no longer negotiable, it is the fundamental requirement'.

Stores (and the 8-10 teams that make them up) compete against other stores and this has instilled a deeply competitive and hard grained work ethic into the culture of the company. This is another confusing element of the story. A 'New Age-ish' culture co-exists with Whole Foods' intensely competitive orientation. In 1992, when the company went public, Mackey announced that Whole Foods was 'going to be an organization based on love instead of fear'. So, Whole Foods has grown into the largest natural foods market in the world, but it is also principled, idealistic and democratic, whilst remaining committed to compensating employees aggressively and rewarding shareholders all at the same time. Non-executive employees hold 94 per cent of company stock options and the company covers 100 per cent of the cost of employee health insurance. And, in one of the numerous transparency and trust-generating policies that define the culture of the company, executive salaries are limited to 14 times the average employee's salary. Contrast this with the figure cited by Drucker in the last years of his life, when he warned the American business community that, at about 431 times the average worker salary, CEO pay in the US was becoming dangerously out of balance. Of course, the company founder Mackey and others close to him hold generous amounts of company stock and are thus wealthy without the salaries they receive. The point here, though, is that there is more to the story than money.

A 'New Age-ish' culture co-exists with Whole Foods' intensely competitive orientation.

The limit on executive salaries is not just talk. Mackey is committed to what he calls 'no secrets management'. Acting on this, he places 'the pay book', which details

Mackey is committed to what he calls 'no secrets management'.

the salaries and bonuses paid to all of the company's employees, in the main office of each store. This way, there are no secrets about who is earning what. As a publicly traded company, the extent to which Whole Foods shares information with its employees is unusual: 'Whole Foods supports teamwork with a wide-open financial system. It collects and distributes information to an extent that would be unimaginable almost anywhere else. Sensitive figures on store sales, team sales, profit margins, even salaries, are available to every person in every location. In fact the company shares so much information that the SEC designated all… employees insiders for stock trading purposes.'

Charles Fishman summarizes the Whole Foods Management Philosophy as one premised on 'Democracy and Discipline'. It consists of four key dimensions:

1. *All work is teamwork.* By giving teams the power to hire and fire new team members, there is an immediacy and energy to work at Whole Foods that is very often missing at other companies. This, combined with the company's 'gainsharing' programme, which ties team performance to team bonuses, means that for 'retail work' the company's employees can be compensated very well. The more productive your new recruits (measured by sales divided by labour per hour), the more money the team earns. This openness, and even toughness, is supported by the 'pay book' policy, which aims to have nothing hidden from employees, all of whom are asked to be tough and competitive team players. This lies at the heart of what Fishman means when he says that the company's 'values are soft-hearted' but its 'competitive logic is hard-headed'.

2. *Anything worth doing is worth measuring.* Whole Foods' open management approach is not meant only to demonstrate to its employees that management is open and honest. It is also about making all data - for measurement purposes - available all the time. No one can hide from poor performance. As Mackey says, 'In most companies... management controls information and therefore controls people. By sharing information, we stay aligned to the vision of a shared fate'. This notion of a 'shared fate' has become a mantra for Mackey and the company's top leadership.

3. *Be your own toughest competitor.* 'Competition is ubiquitous at Whole Foods', writes Charles Fishman. Teams within stores compete with each other, stores with other stores and regions with other regions. This is the source of all the readily available performance data. 'Pressure for performance', Fishman suggests, 'comes from peers rather than from headquarters, and it comes in the form of internal competition'. Stores are measured in 'store tours' by groups of employees from other stores and in what are called 'The Customer Snapshot' (TCS) reviews, wherein members from company headquarters visit stores, shop for 300 different items and rate the stores accordingly. Unlike the Store Tours, the TCS reviews are unannounced visits. They provide yet another source of data on how well stores are performing.

4. *Sustainable success.* Taken together, the other three core ingredients (teamwork, competition and measurement) of the Whole Foods management philosophy are aimed at building a sustainable organization, both in terms of its

human-centred employee practices and policies *and* its larger positioning in the market place, in society and in the ecosystem of a 'post-capitalist society'. The holism that lies at the centre of the Whole Foods story is unmistakable and, while the company likes to talk about sustainable success, it is equally a story of constant innovation and humanism that happens to be taking place in a business organization.

6.5   John Mackey on 'Control'

Of course Whole Foods is not alone in having built a human-centred and decentralized business that is also intensely competitive and financially successful. In a recent *Strategy & Business* article, 'Ricardo Semler Won't Take Control', Lawrence Fisher writes about the management practices at Semco and the much cited example of participative, democratic management pioneered by the company's chairman and principal shareholder, Ricardo Semler. Enough has been written about Semco, and by Semler himself, that I don't need to rehearse the whole Semco story here. In the article, Fisher describes the extent to which Semler practises a form of hands-off management that would be virtually unacceptable just about anywhere else, including at Southwest Airlines or Whole Foods. The important commonality here, between Semco, Southwest and Whole Foods, relates to *control*.

Like Herb Kelleher, who celebrates being 'behind his employees' (in terms of not being 'in the know' with regards to all that they are doing), and Semler's insistence that he cannot possibly know all that's going on in the company and does not pretend to know, John Mackey practices his own form of hands-off and decentralized management. There is a trend towards centralization

Mackey (like Semler and Kelleher) celebrates the extent to which the company runs without his input.

under way at Whole Foods at the present time, marked by more centralized buying of some products across store locations, but much sourcing is still done locally, particularly of local and organic produce, meats, etc. Also, the 'national leadership training programme' is becoming an increasingly centralized element of the company's management system. Even factoring in these types of programmes and practices, Mackey (like Semler and Kelleher) celebrates the extent to which the company runs without his input. Some employees would certainly disagree with this characterization of Mackey's role in the company, as he is very much on top of many aspects of the company's operational details. He is much more plugged in to the day-to-day operations of the company than Ricardo Semler ever has been. The point, though, is that there is a trust and respect that permeates the company and which many employees cite as the central quality of the company's culture that keeps them there and engaged.

Whole Foods' National Leadership Team consists of 24 people, about which Mackey says: 'We make decisions by majority vote. I almost never overrule them'. In his article on Mackey's leadership style, Charles Fishman suggests that Mackey 'doesn't just delegate, in fact, he can seem almost diffident about his company'. In the interview, Fishman asks Mackey how the 140 cashiers at one store are able to maintain their mellow and customer-calming effect as they juggle shift changes, job sharing, scheduling and customer loyalty-building and rapport-building efforts. Mackey responds like a confused college professor. 'That does sound like a problem... A team that large could confound the basic operating principle. But I'll tell you, I don't have the faintest idea how they've solved that problem. That's not my job anymore. But call them up, ask. I guarantee they have found a solution. I'd be curious to know what it is'. Yet, as with Semler's hands-off approach to management (which is not Mackey's approach exactly, to be sure), management gurus rarely praise this sort of participative management style. Within the traditional perspective on what constitutes 'proper management control', and despite the fact that in purely financial terms participative management can prove to be effective, there remains something 'subversive' if not mildly annoying about this type of managerial style. You can't do it like that! But if the bottom-line results are there, which is ostensibly what the traditionalist objection is based on, then what's the gripe? What is so subversive and radical about 'making money' in a different (and innovative) way? I've yet to come across a response to this basic question that I really understand.

6.6   The New Pragmatism

Whole Foods embodies and represents what I refer to as the 'win-win capitalism' of a New Pragmatism. Businesses can be highly successful financially *and* humanistic *and* environmentally conscious at the same time.

Perhaps more so than the other firms considered here, Whole Foods embodies and represents what I refer to as the 'win-win capitalism' of a New Pragmatism. Businesses can be highly successful financially *and* humanistic *and* environmentally conscious at the same time. It is happening all the time and many of these companies are intensely innovative in their industries as a simple matter of fact. It is not the financial success, per se, that traditionalists object to. They object to the way that the riches of the New Pragmatists are won. It smacks of the 1960s, of the Summer of Love and all that. It turns out, though, that alternative methods can also provide the framework and foundation for an entirely new and winning formula for management practice. It starts with a basic humanism, which is applied equally in the employee space and the consumer space, is principled and idealistic, but which is also competitive and profit oriented. These are the types of criteria that the annual 'Fast 50' awards at *Fast Company* magazine focus on. While it may seem weird and radical to traditionalists, it is just business as usual for the *Fast Company* generation.

For example, Whole Foods has recently reviewed its policies for sourcing animals for its stores' meat departments, with an eye to buying only from farmers who raise animals humanely and to pressuring existing suppliers to change their practices to be more humane. One particular case concerning a farm in California where the company buys its ducks has prodded the company to engage in a total rethink of its animal sourcing policies. At a recent industry conference Mackey was heckled by an animal rights activist about the conditions on the farms where the company sourced some of its meat. The heckler was removed from the event, but she managed to get Mackey's attention. Later, to her surprise, he contacted her and told her she was right and that he wanted to meet with her to talk about what the company could do to address her concerns. They met, and the meeting has set the company on a course to change its sourcing policies altogether. This has forced other suppliers, some of whom rely significantly on their Whole Foods contracts, to change the way they treat their animals before they are sold on to Whole Foods.

In early 2006 Whole Foods bought 458,000 megawatts of renewable energy credits from wind farms throughout the country. This is enough renewable energy to 'offset 100 per cent of the electricity used in all of its stores, warehouses, baking operations, distribution centres, regional offices, and national headquarters in the US and Canada'. It was the largest single wind energy credit ever and it makes Whole Foods the only Fortune 500 company to purchase enough renewable energy credit to equal its electricity use. In a similar type of substantive commitment to its idealism, Mackey has committed $10m/year to support organic, local farms in various parts of the US. Only about 22 per cent of the food sold at Whole Foods comes from large corporate farms, the rest coming from the smaller, organic farmers that the company aims to support. There are some 2,400 organic farmers in this network.

Many companies, to be sure, are pursuing similar types of sustainable practice today. It would be wrong to suggest that Whole Foods is unique in this respect. However, these external, community-focused activities are only a small part of the larger human-centred agenda to which Whole Foods, as a company, is committed.

Finally, I would be remiss if I did not mention here the controversial comments made by Whole Foods' CEO John Mackey in the run up to the company's proposed acquisition of their competitor, Wild Oats. Mackey posted comments on an online financial message board as if he were an anonymous participant in the exchange. Critics have accused him of trying to affect the price that the company would pay for Wild Oats. At the time of writing, The Federal Trade Commission is investigating the matter. Mackey has not denied that he posted the comments. It would be hard for anyone to defend these actions. At the same time, it does nothing to take away from Whole Foods as an organization, or as Peter Drucker would have said, as an instrument of society. It remains an important organization in our society, notwithstanding the events mentioned here. Whole Foods is important, both for the social idealism that it represents as an organization and as an example of a profitable business that stands for things other than just money. One mistake (even if a large one) does not undo the leadership legacy that John Mackey is building as a successful baby boomer CEO working within the New Pragmatism.

7 Stimulating Customer Experience at Starbucks

7.1 Café Culture

Coffee is the second most valuable traded commodity in the world, with an annual trade of about $70bn. It is second only to petroleum. Over 400 billion cups of coffee are consumed annually. More and more of these cups are being served in coffee shops and cafés throughout the world, which interestingly is a return to the original context in which coffee was served and consumed hundreds of years ago. First in the Arab world, spreading from Northeast Africa across Yemen to the Arabian Peninsula in the 9th century, coffee was consumed and appreciated originally as a stimulant. Its invigorating properties were recognized in the Arab world in the 10th-12th centuries as a conversational stimulant and men began to gather to drink coffee and debate the issues of the day. As coffee houses spread into Europe, they took on the same significance as gathering places for debate and conversation, acquiring the name of 'penny universities' in Europe. The coffee house as a social locale for conversation, debate and philosophy was controversial at different points in time, as were the intoxicating effects of coffee when consumed in large quantities. In the early 16th century in Mecca, for example, coffee consumption was criminalized, which highlighted the potentially 'subversive' nature of both the 'buzz' and the conversation that accompanied it.

7.2 Coffee in the US and Britain

Until the last couple of decades, coffee and coffee consumption in the US and UK have been benign. And bland! As Mark Pendergrast discusses in his book on the history of coffee, *Uncommon Grounds*, a combination of volatile commodity prices, two world wars and the style-crushing blandness of 1950s Modernism conspired to make coffee both tasteless and boring at mid-century. Concerned with stretching coffee as far as possible to save money meant that coffee was brewed with too much water, producing a thin taste that did not inspire enthusiasm for the drink or for any of the cultural context that surrounds coffee consumption in many parts of the world.

And then came the dreaded 1960s and 1970s! Traditionalists felt like this was the end of the world. But the leaders of the cultural transformation, the baby boomers, captured much of the idealism of that era when they settled down and got serious about their families and careers. This settling down process provides the backdrop for the 'experience economy' as we know it *and* has transformed the larger economy over the past twenty-five years. In this sense, the 1960s and 1970s also ushered in a business revolution. There would never have been a Whole Foods, Innocent Drinks or Starbucks before the 'cultural revolution' of that period. Nor, for that matter, the West's current passion for fresh foods, produce, wines, micro brews and organic foods generally. Now that Wal-Mart, Asda, Tesco and Sainsbury's have all begun to sell organic/ foodie products to increasingly idealistic customers, the revolution is complete - what was once 'far out' is the new common sense.

7.3   Enter Starbucks

Thus the market space was created for Starbucks. As at Whole Foods, it is unlikely that an Italian style coffee house serving $2.00 coffees and $4.00 speciality coffees could have found a home (outside of hippy enclaves such as Boulder, North Beach and Madison) until after the sixties. That is because Starbucks is in the *experience*

Starbucks is in the *experience* business more than it is the coffee business, per se.

business more than it is the coffee business, per se. Like other companies that sell encounters and experiences that accompany the purchase of products (the Body Shop, REI, Pottery Barn and Anthropologie, for example), you need customers ready to pay for that experience. It is important to understand Starbucks's approach to innovation in the larger cultural context in which it has matured. Its understanding of the cultural pulse of consumer markets, perhaps implicitly at first but now more explicitly, has kept the company at the cutting edge of innovation for its entire history.

Unfortunately for Starbucks, its success has also made it a large target for criticism. A group of independent coffee shop owners has engaged Starbucks in a bitter class action lawsuit based on the claim that the company engages in monopolistic practices. The suit, which began with a small, independent coffee house in Seattle, has grown over the past few years to include several other small firms, each making the same basic claim against Starbucks. An attorney representing one of the first plaintiffs in the case describes their claim thus: 'We contend that Starbucks's market practices are more about destroying competition than pouring a good cup of coffee... It is clear to us that Starbucks's game plan is to completely dominate a market by forcing out competition, something they've done quite well in the Seattle area'. The relative merits of this claim are beyond the scope of this chapter and this book, though I am aware that some people would strongly disagree with this position.

The scale of Starbucks's *business* success, though, speaks for itself. It currently operates around 12,000 stores in 37 countries, has a market capitalization of $20-$25bn, gross revenues of $8bn, operating margins of around 10 per cent and net income of $650m. It is by far the largest retailer of speciality coffee in the world and, like Southwest Airlines in low cost air travel and Whole Foods in the natural grocery market, it has largely defined the speciality coffee space for modern consumers. In this respect Starbucks is an industry-defining innovator. Howard Schultz, Starbucks's Chairman and CEO, insists that the company does not take this success for granted and that the company constantly works to earn its customers' respect and loyalty. And, as I discuss throughout this chapter, it continues to innovate in new directions on a regular basis.

7.4   Innovation at Starbucks

We'll rarely talk about the product... Starbucks is a place that allows the customer experience to happen. Things in the store are just props in the experience.
Starbucks's VP of Beverages

At the heart of Starbucks's success lie two essential types of innovation: one internal and one external.

At the heart of Starbucks's success lie two essential types of innovation: one internal and one external. Externally, Starbucks has largely defined the coffee house experience for a mass consumer audience throughout the world. While independent coffee houses obviously existed before Starbucks, its intense focus on both the quality and taste of its coffees as well as on the ambience of the coffee house experience - in design, architecture, aesthetics, music, etc. - has increased competition and raised the bar for coffee houses and cafés everywhere. Despite the criticism that Starbucks receives, particularly from small coffee shops, one would be naïve to think that the industry space itself, as we know it today, would have been possible without a Starbucks. Not only has Starbucks increased competition in terms of forcing ever-higher qualities of coffee to be served in coffee houses everywhere, but also the very cultural practice and consumer habit of the coffee house experience has been defined largely by the Starbucks brand.

The second critical innovation in the Starbucks story, similar to some of the other cases discussed here, is the innovative and progressive way it treats and manages its employees. Starbucks is a retail business (almost 80 per cent of its sales come from its retail locations) and its employees are communicators of the company's values, brand and identity. This entails numerous specific commitments by the company to its employees, including its approach to providing health insurance, its approach to compensation and the opportunities it provides to employees for training and development. Also, like the other companies discussed in the book, Starbucks is becoming increasingly committed to social idealism and corporate social responsibility in specific ways that further connect the values of its employees and management with those of its customers. This type of value-alignment between internal and external constituents is a powerful driver of brand loyalty and brand equity for the company.

Value-alignment between internal and external constituents is a powerful driver of brand loyalty and brand equity.

7.5   Starbucks Office

A recent article in *Wired* magazine, 'Café 2.0: After the Gold Rush', talks about the role of the coffee shop and, in the particular case of Ritual Coffee Roasters in San Francisco, about the role of the coffee shop in the lives of Web 2.0 companies. Ritual Coffee Roasters was an early example of the coffee shop turned co-working space. In the past few years it has played host to brainstorming entrepreneurs from Flickr and Netflix, offering a social place to gather, share ideas and feed off the collective energy of a 'contemporary penny university'. While not all coffee shops host such A-list web entrepreneurs, the process of visioning, dreaming and planning for imagined futures does unfold (with varying degrees of success) at coffee shops around the world. Particularly for business people who travel regularly for their work, the ubiquitous

Coffee shops (like Starbucks) are becoming extensions of a postmodern workplace.

nature of Starbucks in most metropolitan markets means that a Wi-Fi enabled Starbucks as a mobile office is never very far away. In this way, for both busy people travelling for their work and for those within local markets building their own companies, coffee shops (like Starbucks) are becoming extensions of a postmodern workplace.

Now with over 12,000 stores worldwide in some 37 countries, the number of work-related conversations taking place at Starbucks is inestimable. Stimulated, both chemically by the caffeine and culturally and aesthetically via design and music, salespeople are connecting with customers; programmers are writing code; graphical user interface (GUI) designers are mapping new customer experiences; ad people are conceiving new campaigns and young MBAs are cooking up new ways to make money. With Wi-Fi access now available in most locations, and with Bluetooth and Blackberry in tow, office networking is virtually total.

7.6   Starbucks Music

For regular Starbucks customers, one of the signature elements of the experience is the music. The music at Starbucks is now streamed through its own satellite radio channel, 'Hear Music', which is managed by 'musicologists' who have broad ranging and eclectic tastes. It is not unusual at all for me to sit in a Starbucks for a couple of hours and not hear *one* familiar song. It is hard for me to imagine that there is that much music out there, but apparently there is and Hear Music brings it to the customer. The music loops on air at Starbucks connect with customers in subtle yet powerful ways. It is not a random connection, either. Through in-depth, ethnographic analysis and mining for customer interests and aspirations, the company has committed itself to knowing its customers in an intimate way. Customer

Through in-depth, ethnographic analysis and mining for customer interests and aspirations, the company has committed itself to knowing its customers in an intimate way.

insight and innovation go hand in hand in the way the company designs the Starbucks experience. Recently ranked the 9th most innovative company in the US by *Business Week*, Starbucks puts into action very explicitly the combination of ethnography, observation, design and innovation I discussed earlier.

Since 2002 the company has hired outside ethnographers to observe and interact with customers to better understand them in order to further refine the coffee house experience for them. In 2005, the company dispatched a group of product development and cross-company teams on 'inspirational field trips' to various parts of Europe - Paris, Düsseldorf and London - to better understand and connect with distinct cultural contexts in their European markets. This type of explicitly anthropological research, conducted by Starbucks employees, is an example of Christopher Alexander's seemingly simplistic focus on the 'science of observation': pay close, unbiased attention to what is actually going on and what people are actually doing. Understanding the in-context behaviour of customers is a stock in trade for the design industry and here Starbucks is employing its own version of consumer observation to improve its design of customer experience.

Understanding the in-context behaviour of customers is a stock in trade for the design industry.

The music that one hears at Starbucks (now available at Hear Music on XM Satellite Radio) is but a gateway into the company's vision of itself as an aggregator and purveyor of music. For sale in stores are compilations of songs, chosen by famous musicians who are asked to list the songs that have inspired them in their own careers. These include CDs of songs compiled by the Rolling Stones, Sheryl Crow, Emmylou Harris and others. They provide a glimpse into which musicians have inspired the albums that are being played on Hear Music. Paul McCartney's new album, for example, was actually produced by Hear Music and is being distributed at Starbucks locations throughout the world. Starbucks

Regardless of its success in its music venture, the venture itself is important in that it is an enactment of *iterative innovation*, wherein the company is constantly seeking out new things, new ideas, new experiences for its customers.

wants to evolve into a portal, a distributor of music, adding a deeper dimension to the Starbucks experience. Regardless of its success in its music venture, the venture itself is important in that it is an enactment of *iterative innovation*, wherein the company is constantly seeking out new things, new ideas, new experiences for its customers. This is what Roger Martin refers to, in his outline of the design-centric firm, as *abductive thinking* - that is, an embrace of what might be and not simply an optimization of what already is! What else might be possible inside Starbucks? The openness to an unknown future and the willingness to experiment suggest that new things will always be forthcoming from Starbucks. This openness to emergent opportunities is a key source of 'differentiation' and excitement at Starbucks.

The idea behind the latest iteration of Starbucks Music, which is currently operational in selected markets, is to build kiosks for listening to music and for CD burning into the design of selected stores. Designed in different ways - some like a sit-down bar at a pub and others like the walk-up kiosks at a Virgin Super Store - the idea is to allow customers to listen to a collection of some 300,000 songs, from which they can choose whatever songs they want, pay by the song and then have those songs burned on to a disc while they wait (and have a cup of coffee, of course). While customer take-up of the services has been slower than the company had anticipated, there is no shortage of ambition in Schultz's strategic vision.

> We are the most frequented retailer in the world [the average customer goes to a store 18 times a month]...With hundreds of thousands of songs digitally filed and stored, these Hear Music coffee shops (which is what they are being called), combined with our existing locations, can become the largest music store in any city we have a Starbucks in. And because of the traffic

[40 million customers pass through Starbucks each week], the frequency, and the trust that our customers have in the experience and the brand, we believe strongly that we can transform the retail record industry.

Is it really possible for Starbucks to transform/translate the scale of its brand into primary spaces beyond coffee? Schultz certainly thinks so. 'Great companies are defined by their discipline and their understanding of who they are and who they are not', Schultz says, 'But also, great companies must have the courage to examine strategic opportunities that are transformational - as long as they are not inconsistent with the guiding principles and values of the core business'. To date, perhaps the most transformational move the company has made has been its aggressive move into music. With the stated goal of being the largest retailer of music in the world, Schultz and company are talking about morphing into a new kind of über-brand. The key to this step was the acquisition of Hear Music, the California based record chain that already had a musical style and ambience that Schultz felt resonated with the Starbucks experience. That marriage has been a key driver of Starbucks's larger push into music.

Schultz describes the move into music as a natural evolution.

Schultz describes the move into music as a natural evolution. For many years, Schultz recalls, customers have stopped employees and asked, 'What song is this?', in a tone suggesting that the customer liked the song but had never heard it. 'When I saw Hear Music for the first time', Schultz recalls, 'it was clear that they had cracked the code on the sense of discovery that music should have. We never dreamed that we'd be sitting on the unique opportunity we're sitting on now. We just saw that they were doing for music what we had done for coffee. It was this very respectful way of presenting music that, in a way, had become a lost art'. It was five years between the acquisition of Hear Music and the roll out of their first 'combination store', where music is available to sample, burn and buy. Some have questioned why it took the company so long to make something out of the Hear Music acquisition. 'Sometimes I think when you make an acquisition like this, it's not necessarily for what you're thinking of today; its something you're going to learn and incubate into the company.'

Part of that long-term vision is the recognition that in a post-Napster/iTunes music industry that is rapidly being disintermediated, new solutions to copyrighting and purchasing music are still on the horizon. Also, and importantly, Starbucks aims to be a provider of musical discovery for a slightly older Bobo market, which is not the market at which the thrust of the traditional music industry is directed. Like many other areas across the mass marketing universe, traditional music marketing, such as it is, is targeted at 15-30 year olds. Many of Starbucks's most loyal customers are between 25 and 50. They possess a different and more nuanced history of listening to music and they have more disposable income. Many of the albums this demographic wants to hear are by artists of their generation and may not be played very regularly on FM radio stations. This 'reconnect' between the older demographic and the music of their generation can be a powerful source of brand loyalty among Bobos.

According to some observers, Schultz is not so much transformational in his thinking as he is pragmatic. Geoffrey Moore, author of numerous books on strategic management (including, most recently, *Dealing with Darwin*), suggests that Schultz is acutely aware that the market for expensive, upscale coffee will not continue to grow forever. 'His market is not all coffee drinkers. His market is people who buy into an upscale 21st century café society experience, which is much smaller.' Supporting this view, Adrian Slywotzky, of Mercer Management

> Importantly, Starbucks aims to be a provider of musical discovery for a slightly older Bobo market, which is not the market at which the thrust of the traditional music industry is directed.

Consultants, suggests that Schultz is 'already looking ahead, doing the arithmetic and saying, "Well, our current model is not forever!". There are probably a few more years of growth left in coffee shops, and he's asking, "How do we manage the inevitable slowdown a couple of years from now?".'

Most successful entrepreneurs must balance risk management with a vision that is realistic. More fundamentally, Starbucks is willing to change, evolve and *innovate*.

Schultz is pragmatic, to be sure, as most successful entrepreneurs must balance risk management with a vision that is realistic. More fundamentally, Starbucks is willing to change, evolve and *innovate*. Music is one concept that has occupied the company's imagination for much of the early 2000s. But there are already others in the making. Recently, the company has upped its interests in, and commitments to, initiatives around social and cultural responsibility and films. Talk now is that Howard Schultz wants to add movies to the agenda of a more media-oriented Starbucks.

7.7   Starbucks Media

How far Starbucks will be able to grow into a 'media company' is unclear. Surely there are many shareholders who would rather not find out. Whether one sees it as visionary, pragmatic or crazy, it will be at least a few years until the company has enough data to know whether 'leveraging the Starbucks brand across multiple channels' will be successful. Nonetheless, the company is not waiting idly by to see the results before trying out the next thing. The company's latest 'prototyping' also pushes in the direction of media, with its current experimentation as a distributor of books and film. Mitch Albom, author of the fictional self-help best-seller, *Tuesdays with Morrie*, has signed an agreement with Starbucks to distribute and cross-promote his latest novel, *For One More Day*. He will promote the book with in-store signings in 25 cities, where he will also promote a literacy programme that has been authored by the company. Of the deal, Albom says, 'I am honoured that Starbucks has chosen my book, and I am proud to support any effort that helps bring people together to read'. Schultz sees this sort of event, like listening to and discovering music, as a natural extension of the Starbucks experience. 'Community is incredibly important to Starbucks. Our goal is to support the discovery and enjoyment of Mitch's new book, by leveraging what is so special about the Starbucks in-store environment.'

Schultz sees, as his many critics like to point out, almost limitless possibilities in terms of how the company can extend its brand in new ways. The company has recently promoted the 'socially conscious' film, *Akeelah and the Bee*, a movie about a young African American girl who overcomes stacked odds to reach the finals of a national spelling bee. 'Our customer is the demographic that Hollywood needs as it is facing a double-digit decline in the box office and slowing DVD sales...We have a unique cross-section of assets - a foundation of trust and confidence in Starbucks - that can promote a movie that our customers know is relevant.' In-store promotions aimed at exposing Starbucks's customers to 'new cultural opportunities' are, according to the company, just in their infancy. Ken Lombard, head of Starbucks's Entertainment division, is seeking out new scripts and new 'cultural opportunities' to support and promote. Successful or not, it is clear that there is no fear of the unknown at Starbucks. Not content simply to 'manage the known', the company has clearly committed itself to 'building an unknown' future, premised on innovation, design and customer-centric growth. A significant part of this growth is also internally driven in the way it recruits, compensates and promotes employees. In addition, Starbucks's internal, employee-centred commitments are part of the innovation equation.

Schultz sees almost limitless possibilities in terms of how the company can extend its brand in new ways.

7.8   Internal Innovation at Starbucks

A 2002 *Strategy & Business* article outlines Starbucks's road to success as being defined by 'relational capital', which refers to the connections and commitments of the company to four key constituencies: customers, suppliers, alliance partners and employees. Of these four sources of relational capital in the company, its relationship with its employees is where I want to focus the discussion now. Similar to that at Whole Foods, the Starbucks experience is an interface with both a consciously 'built environment' and a 'human environment'. It is in the specific policies for, and commitments to, its employees that the internal and external environments of the Starbucks brand intersect and are defined.

At the centre of Starbucks's relational capital rests the company's comprehensive commitments to the well-being of its employees. Schultz articulates this commitment in a matter of fact way: 'We can be extremely profitable and competitive, with a highly regarded brand, and also be respected for treating our people well… In the end, it's not only possible to do both, but you can't really do one without the other.' Many unapologetically compete for market success while they treat their employees poorly, if not with outright contempt. In the language of management theory, most companies operate under a set of assumptions that Douglas McGregor once referred to as Theory X: that is, the assumption that people /employees do not intrinsically like work, are naturally lazy, can only be motivated to work by carrots and sticks and generally need to be treated like children. In this sort of corporate environment, which sadly remains pervasive in many businesses throughout the world, work can be a degrading activity. This is not the case at Starbucks.

Schultz, like John Mackey and Herb Kelleher, starts with a different set of assumptions about people and work,

'Relational capital' refers to the connections and commitments of the company to four key constituencies: customers, suppliers, alliance partners and employees.

It is in the specific policies for, and commitments to, its employees that the internal and external environments of the Starbucks brand intersect and are defined.

Theory X is the assumption that people /employees do not intrinsically like work, are naturally lazy, can only be motivated to work by carrots and sticks, and generally need to be treated like children.

Theory Y is the belief that people can and will engage in their work with passion if they are given something meaningful to do, some autonomy to do it, and are generally treated like adults.

which McGregor referred to as Theory Y. Theory Y is the belief that people can and will engage in their work with passion if they are given something meaningful to do, some autonomy to do it and are generally treated like adults. 'Our mission statement about treating people with respect and dignity is not just words but a creed we live by every day. You can't expect your employees to exceed the expectations of your customers if you don't exceed the employee's expectations of management. That's the contract.' For Schultz this is personal. 'It wasn't until I discovered Starbucks that I realized what it means when your work truly captures your heart and your imagination', he says. Schultz often reflects on how his father, a truck driver in New York City, once lost his job and left the family without any benefits or financial security of any kind. His long-term commitment to providing a human-centred context for Starbucks's employees to work in stems from the convictions he has had most of his life.

For a start, Starbucks was one of the first companies in the retail sector to offer full health benefits to part-time workers. It also offers benefits to same or opposite sex partners of full- or part-time employees, which includes comprehensive health benefits, medical care, prescriptions, dental and vision coverage and other preventative care. Soft-hearted HR policies coexist with hard-nosed competition in the market, which is a textbook case of a 'virtuous spiral organization'. Other offerings provided by the company to employees include:

Soft-hearted HR policies coexist with hard-nosed competition in the market, which is a textbook case of a 'virtuous spiral organization'.

- Retirement savings plans

- Discounted stock options (called 'Bean Stock')

- Income protection plans

- Adoption assistance plans

- Management bonus plans

- Support resources for child care

- Support resources for elder care.

According to one study by *Fortune* magazine, Starbucks ranked second in a list of companies with the most generous employment benefits packages in the country. It has one of the lowest employee turnover rates in the food and beverage industry, which is 250 per cent lower than the industry average.

Also, while any global company requires a significant amount of standardization, coordination and centralization, the company follows a philosophy of decentralization as much as it feels is possible. Baristas, the women and men who make and serve coffee drinks to customers, interact with customers every day and are seen by the company as ambassadors of the Starbucks brand. The company spends relatively little money on advertising and the interface with customers is their most important type of advertising. Each store relies on the personalities and connections between baristas and customers and less on canned advertizing produced at the national level. In this seemingly simple commitment, each store's success is, to some extent, local and personal. Giving employees a role and, in some cases, an ownership stake in the success of the brand and the individual store, is a source of motivation and engagement for employees. In an industry where turnover is rampant, and where apathy often defines the customer interface, Starbucks offers a refreshing alternative. The employment brand at Starbucks is consonant with the consumer brand and the alignment between internal and external constituencies is a defining feature of the company's human-centred identity.

Each store's success is, to some extent, local and personal.

7.9　Customer Experience Rules

Given the nature of the in-store work and the age profile of the company's employees, there are inherent limits to how low the attrition numbers can go. Starbucks's primary innovative thrust has to be external, in the brand equity of the Starbucks experience. That innovation, though, should not be underestimated. The impact that the company is having far and wide, across many sectors of the economy that seek to connect culturally with customers, is astounding. How many companies get their customers to visit their stores 18 times a month? Consider the Starbucks effect in the slogans written up recently in *Fast Company* magazine, where companies from various sectors now aspire to be the 'Starbucks of their respective industry':

> 'We have become known as the Starbucks of flowers' *KaBloom web site*

> 'Savor a HoneyBaked Ham, the Starbucks of the ham business' *eHow.com*

> 'Cereality wants to be the Starbucks of the breakfast bowl' *Business 2.0*

> 'The Post is becoming the Starbucks of saloons' *Detroit Free Press.*

With a highly popular satellite radio station on XM Satellite radio, in-store music experiences and cross promotions in film and book publishing, Starbucks increasingly interacts with customers and potential customers across an expanding range of cultural experiences. Relating the relentless innovation at the heart of Starbucks to Howard Schultz's personal energy and drive, one management consultant says that 'exceptional leaders cultivate the Merlin-like habit of acting in the present moment as ambassadors of a radically different future, in order to

Starbucks increasingly interacts with customers and potential customers across an expanding range of cultural experiences.

imbue their organizations with a breakthrough vision of what is possible to achieve'. In many ways the core of Starbucks's success is precisely the type of 'future mining' that Roger Martin has called for in terms of abductive, 'what if?' thinking.

7.10   Starbucks's Virtuous Spiral

By continually innovating, and by constantly reinvigorating the brand and its experience, both employees and consumers are energized. This is Starbucks's virtuous spiral and it is all about innovation. For example, when Starbucks recently acquired a bottled water company with a starting goal of contributing 5 cents from every bottle to organizations that provide free water to children in the developing world, the brand and its reach as an institution in society was extended. As one of the most popularly visited 'third places' in U.S. society today, Starbucks is simultaneously growing a massive business and doing good for society. In many respects, Starbucks is a central location, a node in the network, of the New Pragmatism that underlies the combination of a pro-business/pro-society agenda I have been discussing. Traditionalists say it can't (or shouldn't) be done, but they are wrong. Companies like Whole Foods and Starbucks make it a reality every day.

> In many respects, Starbucks is a central location, a node in the network, of the New Pragmatism that underlies the combination of a pro-business/pro-society agenda.

7.11   Schultz's Memo

A recent memo, written by Shultz and dispersed throughout the company and which eventually appeared on the web, underscores many of the themes talked about here. In the memo, which many people at first thought was a hoax, Schultz criticizes Starbucks for having grown too large, too generic and too commoditized - and he laments these things openly in public. The memo, entitled 'The

Shultz is touching here on the point raised by Roger Martin when he talks about heuristics, mysteries and algorithms.

Commoditization of the Starbucks Experience', argues that much of the 'romance and theatre' has been lost from the stores and that the company needs to 'look into the mirror' to make the necessary changes and rediscover a 'passion for the Starbucks experience'. Among other themes, Shultz is touching here on the point raised by Roger Martin when he talks about heuristics, mysteries and algorithms (see Section 1.6). Shultz seems to be lamenting the disappearance of mystery at the company as well as the creeping algorithms that have driven the company's torrid growth over the last decade. Simply being aware of the algorithms that are defining Starbucks does not make them go away. It is difficult to see how Shultz can transcend this dilemma within the context of the coffee house, per se. This would suggest that Starbucks's media ventures - music, literature and film - really are *that* important. Is coffee just a Trojan horse?

8 Google and All the Information in the World

8.1 Über-Innovator

All three of the companies discussed so far were recently ranked within the top 100 'most innovative companies' in the 2005 *Business Week*/Boston Consulting Group rankings. Starbucks was ninth, Southwest Airlines was twenty-fifth and Whole Foods was thirty-sixth. Google, however, was ranked second, behind only Apple.

Google is an 'über-innovator'. The story of Google is, quite simply, a story of innovation. It is the tale of a relentless and opportunistic relationship with *constraints*. Successful innovative cultures deal with constraints - materials, space, time, budgets, personnel, etc. - as challenges rather than as deal killers. As Roger Martin suggested at the outset, a new breed of company, either explicitly or implicitly, is beginning to view the inevitability of constraints as the touchstones of opportunity. Even large industrial conglomerates such as P&G and GE, under the leadership of design- and innovation-focused CEOs Laffley and Immelt respectively, have built a designer's orientation into the way the company deals with constraints and seeks out new opportunities.

From the beginning, Google's *raison d'être* was audacious: to master the digital search environment by creating the definitive application (Page Rank) for ranking the relevance and importance of Web sites as they relate to a search inquiry. Early on, when the Page Rank system was being developed, Sergey Brin and Larry Page, the company's founders, wanted to achieve a level of information cataloguing and retrieval across the global digital network that just about everyone around

> Successful innovative cultures deal with constraints - materials, space, time, budgets, personnel, etc. - as challenges rather than as deal killers.

them said was impossible. Stanford University Professor of Computer Science, Dennis Allison, puts it this way: 'The idea of digitizing the entirety of the universe and making it work was something nobody was willing to tackle but lots of people knew needed to be done'. Innovation at Google has been intensely user-centred ever since its very first innovation, Page Rank, which remains the company's core application and primary vehicle for generating advertising revenue. What do consumers of Web-mediated information want? How do users rank and grade the information and sites that are out there? What new and emergent search-oriented applications are users saying and indicating they want and need?

8.2   Boons not Bombs

To understand how Google systematically innovates for user experience, we must return to the important issue relating to constraints and how design-centric firms use constraints as boons and not bombs. Marissa Mayer, VP for search products and user experience, discusses Google's approach to constraints in an instructive way in a couple of recent interviews. At its core, Google is an engineering company and it has an engineering culture. However, like artists, architects and designers, engineers deal with the balancing act of turning constraints into opportunities. There is a powerfully creative dimension to the succession of Google innovations, such as Google News, Google Maps, Google Earth, Google Pictures, Google Library, Google Ads, Google Scholar, Google Mail and Google Video. New experiences and ways of navigating the world's information are being *created*, built and commercialized all the time at Google: 'Creativity is often misunderstood. People often think of it in terms of artistic work - unbridled, unguided effort that leads to beautiful effect. If you look deeper, however, you'll find that some of the most inspiring art forms - haiku, sonatas,

Innovation at Google has been intensely user-centred ever since its very first innovation, Page Rank.

'Creativity is often misunderstood. People often think of it in terms of artistic work - unbridled, unguided effort that leads to beautiful effect. If you look deeper, however, you'll find that some of the most inspiring art forms - haiku, sonatas, religious paintings - are fraught with constraints'.

religious paintings - are fraught with constraints. They're beautiful because creativity triumphed over the rules. Constraints shape and focus problems and provide clear challenges to overcome as well as inspiration. Creativity, in fact, thrives best when constrained.' Continuing with this message about constraints, Mayer directly addresses Google's reputation as an audacious organization: 'Yet, constraints must be balanced with a healthy disregard for the impossible. Disregarding the bounds of what we know or what we accept gives rise to ideas that are non-obvious, unconventional or simply unexplored. The creativity realized in this balance between constraint and disregard for the impossible is fuelled by passion and results in revolutionary change.'

The challenge that Google, as a company, set for itself in the beginning was twofold:

- To gather and make freely available 'all the information in the world'

- Continuously to innovate in terms of finding new ways to organize and present the information that its users say they need and want.

Early on, Sergey Brin stated the company's goals in typically idealistic language: 'A perfect search engine will process and understand all the information in the world... That is where Google is headed'. The journey, from 1999 when Brin made this statement, to today, when the company reports $13bn in annual revenues and a market capitalization of around $161bn, has been a textbook case in user-centred design and innovation. As Larry Page recently put it, 'through innovation and iteration, Google takes something that works well and improves upon it in unexpected ways'.

Google's recent ability to monetize the millions and millions of searches that cut through the company daily means that it is no longer a whimsical 'Internet play', but now is an economic behemoth that drives the digital economy.

Today, roughly 60 per cent of all searches on the Internet take place through Google, leaving the rest to be shared by Yahoo, Microsoft's MSN, Ask Jeeves and a few others. Thus, despite its youthfulness and college dorm-like atmosphere, the company has clearly been doing something right. Particularly, its recent ability to monetize the millions and millions of searches that cut through the company daily means that it is no longer a whimsical 'Internet play', but now is an economic behemoth that drives the digital economy.

While many Internet companies have premised their business models on providing 'free content', on the one hand, with an advertising-driven, revenue-generating strategy, on the other, Google has taken this model to new heights. In business model terms, this is not necessarily new, as newspapers and magazines have made money in this way for generations. Though Google's approach is different: it is an ad-revenue system on steroids. This is where the $13bn in annual revenues comes from. Google combines the hardware (servers) and the software (the search applications) into a new kind of knowing and doing machine. Every time someone clicks on a search result, or on a sponsored link, 'Google's brain' grows. And that, at the end of the day, is the Googlenaut. It is still morphing into the future.

8.3   GoogleWare and the Google Economy

From the beginning of the journey, Brin and Page have been all about innovation, about doing new things and doing new things differently despite the massive constraints they faced. A key part of this relates to the fact that, for the company's search technology to work the way it does, the company must essentially copy and link to the entire contents of the World Wide Web all the time. That is, it sits on top of the entire Internet, on top of hundreds of millions of websites representing billions of web pages and this number is continuously growing. To be in this position, the company must have massive computing power, which it does. But it has accomplished this massive power in typical Google fashion.

Google's challenge to innovate in this direction came early on, when Brin and Page were working out of their graduate student offices at Stanford. It was 1998 and the database of sites being downloaded on their servers was growing, as were the numbers of both users and new sites coming online. The two graduate computer science students were short on cash. Enter here 'constraint number one': 'Short on cash, they saved money by buying parts, building their own machines, and scrounging around the loading dock [at Stanford] looking for unclaimed computers... After cramming as many computers as they could into Gates 360 [their office at Stanford], they turned Page's dorm room into a data centre.'

As Sergey Brin says, 'We assembled quite a mismatch of things'. David Vise comments that 'they learned a valuable lesson: how very much they could accomplish by assembling and stringing together inexpensive PCs'. The more people used Google search, the more sites entered into the system of known-sites, which increased the number of sites within Google's orbit exponentially, in turn increasing the need for more and more PCs to capture and store that information. So they built more PCs. The combination of the Google Page Rank search software and the Google-built PCs, which now run into the tens of thousands, has created a massive technological organism. This combination has come to be known as Googleware, a hardware/software combination that is constantly growing through the expansion of such Google services as Gmail, Google Maps, Google Earth, etc.

Ever conscious of costs, Brin and Page found that building their own PCs was not only cheaper than buying fully operating PCs, but it also allowed them to purpose-build them from the beginning to do exactly what they wanted them to do. This approach grew directly out of the way they dealt with being cash-strapped in the early days. It was a creative response to the financial constraints that conditioned both 'Googleware' and Google's culture. At the same time, the two still needed capital to buy basic machines and in the earliest days this was what they needed the venture backing for - not for fancy graphic design, bells and whistles, advertising, or the many other things that some Valley companies were splashing on. They kept their noses to the ground, literally building the business one PC at a time.

The idea behind Google's business model has been that its technology – Googleware – should be both the best of its kind in the world and free for users. Its ability to monetize that superior technology, and the unprecedented flow of traffic through the site, gives Google a considerable advantage over any of its would-be rivals. Nevertheless, Google takes nothing for granted and continuously and relentlessly pushes for innovation, for new things and new ways of doing things. It is in the company's blood. Innovation at Google is both a process/methodology and a core cultural value. So I shall first look at the methodological side of Google's continuous flow of innovation, as a user-centred process, premised on the core principles of design and design thinking, which include constant user observation, brainstorming, rapid prototyping, mining of user feedback, beta implementation, refining, rinse and repeat, etc. Marissa Mayer notes that while only 20-40 per cent of new concepts might become commercially viable, you never get to that figure if you don't possess a commitment to innovation as a core ingredient of organizational DNA in the first place. To

Google takes nothing for granted, and continuously and relentlessly pushes for innovation. Innovation at Google is both a process/ methodology, and a core cultural value.

understand the innovation DNA that sits at the centre of the Google organization, it is necessary to look closely at the culture of the company as well. So I consider this dimension of the Google story after I look closely at their (very precise) methodology of innovation.

8.4   GoogleVation

What is exciting (for users) and scary (for competitors) about innovation at Google is that Search was just the beginning. The rest of the Google Economy comes after that and may eventually dwarf Search. Googleware now includes over thirty products, services and applications, with more in the pipeline. These things don't just happen. They result from a very precise, very intelligent process of creation and innovation. Marissa Mayer, recently featured along with 24 other 'Innovation Champions' in *Business Week*, outlines her Nine Notions of Successful Innovation in the following way:

1. *Ideas come from everywhere:* Google expects everyone to innovate, even the finance team.

2. *Share everything you can:* Every idea, every project, every deadline, it's all accessible to everyone on the intranet.

3. *You're brilliant, we're hiring:* Founders Larry Page and Sergey Brin approve hires. They favour intelligence over experience.

4. *A license to pursue dreams:* Employees get a 'free day' each week. Half of new launches come from this '20 per cent time'.

5. *Innovation, not instant perfection:* Google launches early and often, in small beta tests, before releasing widely.

6. *Don't politik, use data:* Mayer discourages the use of 'I like' in meetings, pushing staffers to use metrics.

7. *Creativity loves restraint:* Give people a vision, rules about how to get there and deadlines.

8. *Worry about usage and users, not money:* Provide something simple to use and easy to love. The money will follow.

9. *Don't kill projects, morph them:* There's always a kernel of something good that can be salvaged.

Creativity is highly encouraged at Google, as it is the source of innovation/business at the company, as well as the magnet that draws some of the most intelligent people in the world to work for the company.

There are several important themes here. First, creativity is highly encouraged at Google, as it is the source of innovation/business at the company, as well as the magnet that draws some of the most intelligent people in the world to work for the company. But not just any creativity. Googlers who want to get funding for a new 20 per cent time project have to pass through the 'Marissa Gauntlet'. (I will talk more about 20 per cent time shortly.) A team is given a 10-minute time slot and the concept is presented on a movie-theatre size screen, next to which are enumerated Mayer's critiques as they are transcribed from audio to text. Next to Mayer's comments is a large clock, which counts down the time remaining for the presenting team. Pressure is intentionally placed on the team. Mayer and her colleagues add to and subtract from the pitch in the margins as it unfolds. Meanwhile the clock is ticking. The *Business Week* article referred to it as 'iteration at lightning speed'.

A second theme within Google's innovation methodology is its enthusiastic embrace of constraints, volume and speed. This repeats, almost verbatim, the innovation cycle practiced at IDEO. At Google, keeping constraints right out front is critical. Unlike the managerial 'instincts' of traditional firms, where a *we can't do that because* attitude towards constraints often dominates the thinking, those very barriers are touch points of opportunity. For example, downloading the entire contents of the Web onto stacks of PCs sounds crazy and impossible, but it has now been done. A third theme, which parallels the empathy-building, job-sharing programmes used at Southwest Airlines, the team-work principle used at Whole Foods and the Barista-as-Brand commitment at Starbucks, is Google's reliance on collective work, openly available information and collaboration to get most of its work done: 'Google functions as a single, open social network, where every piece of work is laid bare on the company's intranet. This allows Googlers to look for those working on similar technologies, find relevant expertise, or join projects'. Fourth, and the subject of the next section, is an important observation that can be summed up as follows: innovation as a cultural value, symbolized by 20 per cent time and other specific policies, is both a source of competitive advantage in the digital marketplace and an HR strategy. That is, the life of employees *within* the company is an embodiment of the company's strategy *outside* the firm. Innovation is a recruitment tool, a motivational tool, a loyalty tool and a development tool. The promise of an innovative working life is, among other things, why Google attracts some of the world's smartest engineers and technologists and why it has become one of the smartest companies in the world. And one of the youngest! It is, as David Vise suggests in his book, like a college campus, where fun, cleverness, innovation and market-beating technology come together.

Innovation is a recruitment tool, a motivational tool, a loyalty tool and a development tool.

8.5   Back on Campus

Google's enormous financial success is tied closely to the 'working life' that exists within the company. As Brin and Page wrote in the lengthy prospectus for their Initial

Public Offering (IPO), 'Google is not a conventional company. We do not intend to become one'. At the centre of the Google culture is an academic feel, a campus-like environment filled with young, smart technologists engaged in a process of discovery. Corporate leaders and management gurus often talk about flattened hierarchies, employee empowerment and decentralized decision making, but in most cases this is simply talk. In his article, 'Google's random genius is no accidental strategy. Can it last?', *Financial Times* columnist Simon London contrasts Google's approach to innovation and creativity with the control-oriented and fear-based thinking of traditional management 'wisdom':

> Management gurus have for years been telling companies to abandon the traditional top-down, process-driven approach to strategy. Harness the imagination of employees, they exhort. Don't be afraid to experiment. Create an internal market for ideas. Place bets. Build a 'portfolio' of initiatives from which a winning strategy can emerge. Yet old habits die hard. The strategic planning process remains an annual ritual. Chief executives talk about the need to experiment, then mete out punishment when experiments go wrong, or fail to champion unconventional projects when it matters most.

Consider, again, the example from Southwest Airlines where the 'skunk works' project on a new ticketing system was built out unbeknownst to company management. That group was not fearful of what might happen to them if their 'experiment in innovation' failed. Similarly, at Google, employees have a large Green Light to innovate for the company. Its policy of 20 per cent time, which gives employees one full day a week to work on an innovative project of their own choosing, is a tangible commitment to its employees. As London says, 'interesting projects

Google's policy of 20 per cent time, which gives employees one full day a week to work on an innovative project of their own choosing, is a tangible commitment to its employees.

attract talent, irrespective of whether they have been sanctioned by top management. While some initiatives at Google seem to be driven from the top, the company remains open to the possibility that internal market forces will come up with better decisions than committees.'

A few specific examples help illustrate the way in which fresh and potentially commercial ideas are drawn into Google's innovation orbit. Craig Neville-Manning, a Computer Science Professor at Rutgers University, left academic life to work for Google. The 20 per cent time that symbolized Google's culture of innovation attracted him, of course, but he was equally driven by the idea that his research could lead directly to new products and services. Though it has been somewhat maligned for the past couple of years, he was able to create and push through the 'Marissa Gauntlet' the idea of 'Froogle', the price comparison/online shopping service available through Google.

Krishna Bharat, a PhD in Computer Science from Georgia Tech, came to Google passionate about news and about mashing together disparate sources of online news. This passion has now become Google News. Google News began as a 20 per cent time project and then evolved, with the support of Brin and Page and CEO Eric Schmidt, into a full-on product at the company. 'At Google', Bharat says, 'if something is worth doing, it gets funded'. While traditionally-minded managers might cringe at the idea of giving employees one full day a week to work on a pet project (of their own choosing), at Google this policy helps the company both to recruit top engineers and to drive the creation of new, potentially revenue-generating ideas.

The campus-like feel that pervades Google, as well as the day a week given to employees for research and innovation, is not accidental. Both Brin and Page have parents who are academics, so the feel and flow of academic research and 'the academic life' are familiar to them and things that they intentionally built into the culture of the company. The standard academic practice of giving faculty members one day a week to devote to their research is the inspiration behind their creating the 20 per cent time policy in the company. Also, having both come out of Stanford's PhD programme in computer science, they were in some respects continuing their sense of academic discovery in the founding of Google. In his interviews with Google employees while researching his book on the company, David Vise talked with engineer Joe Beda specifically about how the 20 per cent time works at the 'Google campus'. 'There is a big difference between pet projects being permitted and being encouraged. At Google, it is actively encouraged for engineers to do a 20 per cent project. This isn't a matter of doing something in your spare time, but more of actively making time for it. Heck, I don't have a good 20 per cent project yet and I need one. If I don't come up with something, I'm sure it will negatively impact my review.' Innovation is, in this way, a core performance-evaluation metric, not an add-on. For those labs and teams that successfully bring a new product to market, a significant financial windfall is available. Google recently created 'Founder's Awards', which are multi-million dollar stock awards granted to small research teams that produce the best new ideas. Brin recognizes that such huge innovation awards are rare in the corporate world but, as Vise notes, the idea here is 'to retain brilliant innovators who might otherwise leave, taking their ideas with them'.

It might seem that such intense internal competition for launching successful Google labs, for passing through the Marissa Gauntlet, would lead to overly aggressive behaviour and dysfunction. According to Joe Beda, though, this is not the case. 'The intrapersonal [sic]

> Innovation is a core performance-evaluation metric, not an add-on.

environment at Google is very exciting. When someone comes up with a new idea, the most common response is excitement and a brainstorming session. Politics and who owns what rarely enter into it. I don't think I've seen anyone really raise their voice and get into a huge knock-down-drag-out fight since coming to Google.' Perhaps this is because the pie, or the potential pie, at Google is so large and Googlers feel that there is room for everyone at Google to be successful. At least in part, this is also due to the fact that Google has had a very systematic 'share the wealth' approach to compensation and the issuing of stock options. This was particularly evident in and around the company's IPO, when they shook things up and very loudly announced to the world the full breadth of their idealism.

8.6   Sharethewealth.com

There were numerous aspects of the way in which Google went about its IPO that were not only innovative and unique, but that were perceived as radical and 'undoable'. Consistent with its mission that 'all the information in the world' should be made freely available to Google users, Google was determined that a kind of democratic idealism should also define the way it conducted its IPO. To this effect, they pushed hard to have a 'Dutch auction' to establish the initial list price for the stock, rather than allowing Wall Street underwriters to set the price. Brin and Page resented the existing system of taking companies public, wherein Wall Street investment banks set share prices, gave sweet deals to each other and charged enormous fees for doing this. While in theory the underwriting process was to mitigate the risk to the company involved in the IPO, Google was confident that such 'protection' was not necessary in their case. They wanted no preferential treatment for Wall Street professionals. They wanted anybody and everybody to

Consistent with its mission that 'all the information in the world' should be made freely available to Google users, Google was determined that a kind of democratic idealism should also define the way it conducted its IPO.

be able to buy their stock on the opening day of trading. This enabled individual investors, including many Google employees, to buy as many shares as they could afford, unlike many traditional IPOs where institutional positions acquired huge tracks of stock on day one and in doing so drove the price up. In the Dutch auction process, many Googlers became very wealthy in the first few months (and beyond) after the IPO, when the stock climbed from a list price of $85 to its price as I write, of just above $650 per share.

The IPO was also an occasion to announce Google's idealism to the world. In an open letter, which they called 'An Owners' Manual for Google Shareholders', Brin and Page laid claim to what they felt was a higher moral ground for founding and running a publicly traded company.

A management distracted by a series of short-term targets is as pointless as a dieter stepping on a scale every half hour... In Warren Buffet's words:

> We won't smooth quarterly or annual results -
> If earnings figures are lumpy when they reach
> headquarters, they will be lumpy when they
> reach you... As an investor, you are placing a
> potentially risky long-term bet on the team...
> We believe a well functioning society should
> have abundant, free and unbiased access to high
> quality information. Google therefore has a
> responsibility to the world.

> Our search results are the best we know how to
> produce. We do not accept payment for them or
> for inclusion or more frequent updating. We also
> display advertising, which we work hard to make

relevant, and we label it clearly. This is similar to a well-run newspaper, where the advertisements are clear and the articles are not influenced by the advertisers' payments.

We aspire to make Google an institution that makes the world a better place. We are in the process of establishing the Google Foundation [and] intend to contribute significant resources to the foundation, including employee time and approximately one per cent of Google's equity and profits. We hope some day this institution may eclipse Google itself in terms of overall world impact.

The Google Foundation has recently been founded and capitalized initially at $1.1bn. To lead the foundation, they have hired Dr Larry Brilliant, an epidemiologist and successful technology entrepreneur. Brilliant's strategy is to link together a network of charitable and research organizations to fund programmes focused on global poverty, energy and the environment. This is a lofty set of goals and high-minded social idealism for any company, particularly for one as young as Google. But, like the overt idealism at Whole Foods and Starbucks, it is an essential ingredient of the Google story. For Googlers, Google is an important social (as well as economic) institution. The other side of its now famous motto - 'Don't Be Evil'- is 'Be Good'. Working for Google is appealing to its employees because of its idealism as well as because of its ongoing challenge to innovate. This confirms Jim Collins' earlier remark that a key signature of the current economy is the recognition by progressive organizations that business can and should be an instrument of good in society and not solely a moneymaking machine. For its employees, in addition to the challenge and excitement of being involved in innovation labs, working at Google

For Googlers, Google is an important social (as well as economic) institution.

also means participating in something larger, something that might potentially be huge one day.

8.7   GooglePharma

Related to Google's idealism, and situated somewhere between the company and the foundation, is Google's recent foray into the Human Genome Project. In order to store, map and search the massive database that constitutes the human genome knowledge base, Google's unrivalled (by any organization anywhere in the world, all governments included) computing power is an obvious partner. Brin and Page have begun collaborating with Dr Craig Vinter, one of the research pioneers in the genome research project. 'We need to use the largest computers in the world', Vinter says. 'Larry and Sergey have been excited about giving us access to their computers and their algorithm guys and scientists to improve the process of analysing data. It shows the broadness of their thinking. Genetic information is going to be the leading edge of information that is going to change the world. Working with Google, we are trying to generate a gene catalogue to characterize all the genes on the planet and understand their evolutionary development. Geneticists have wanted to do this for generations.'

The implications of this kind of collaboration, between the gene database and Google, are possibly very important. The resulting information could be used to forecast an individual's potential disease profile, as well as by pharmaceutical companies to generate new gene-based drug therapies. It is the exact kind of proactive and positive usage of search and information technology that Brin and Page envisage for Google's future. Across the company, from its founding search technology to its approach to managing human resources and innovation, from its populist and 'radical' IPO to its social idealism

Google does things that other companies (and their managers) say cannot be done.

and the Google Foundation, Google does things that other companies (and their managers) say cannot be done. Google looks at life's constraints as challenges, not as deal killers. Founded on innovation in the first instance, Google's organizational genes are programmed to adapt and evolve over time. That being the case, it is unclear what Google will become in the long term. Will it successfully digitize all the books in the world's most prestigious libraries, as it is suggesting? If this happens, what will this mean for the future of books, of reading, of learning? These are the sorts of audacious questions that Google loves to ask.

The virtuous spiral of an HCE comes together in a winning formula: earnings growth, market share growth, a buoyant share price and engaged and energized employees.

Not incidentally, the combination of innovation and idealism makes Google a great place to work. In *Fortune* magazine's 2007 list of the '100 Best Places to Work', Google is ranked first, followed by Whole Foods at number 5, Starbucks at number 16 and SAS Institute at number 48. The sense of almost unlimited potential at Google surely feeds employees' enthusiasm, as does the seemingly endless list of perks written about recently in *Fortune*. In each of these cases, and particularly in Google's case, the virtuous spiral of an HCE comes together in a winning formula: earnings growth, market share growth, a buoyant share price and engaged and energized employees. The 'pattern languages' that define Google have produced an organization that is very much 'alive' in a Christopher Alexander sense. And, as is the case with other HCEs, this has translated into market-beating financial success.

9   One Hundred Per Cent Innocent

9.1   105 Per Cent Innocent

It would be misleading to suggest, if only through omission, that user-centred innovation and HCEs are the exclusive domain of American firms. Companies throughout the world, in both developed and developing economies, are growing their businesses according to a human-centred logic. Two intriguing and illustrative examples of this are Innocent Drinks in the UK and the upscale luxury brand/fashion designer, Shanghai Tang, in Hong Kong. Each firm, in distinctly different ways, is charting a course defined by customer insight, user-centred innovation and explosive growth.

In a recent *Fast Company* article, 'Give Them Something to Talk About', Chip and Dan Heath (authors of *Made to Stick: Why Some Ideas Survive and Others Die*), suggest that companies capable of sparking conversations *with* and *between* customers have a competitive advantage over brands and companies that simply speak *to* customers. They call it the '105 per cent rule'. All other things being equal, how can one brand stand out as unique and special in a market place crowded with competition? Delivering that 5 per cent more is actually rare, according to the Heaths, and those businesses that manage to deliver that differentiation have a much better chance at building a profitable and durable brand.

One of the examples that the Heaths cite in the article is Innocent Drinks Ltd., the UK maker of all-natural fruit smoothies. According to the Heaths, Innocent has a 'talkable personality', something that resonates in the market and continues to bring people back for more smoothies. In one Innocent campaign called 'Supergran',

Companies capable of sparking conversations *with* and *between* customers have a competitive advantage over brands and companies that simply speak *to* customers.

Innocent has a 'talkable personality', something that resonates in the market and continues to bring people back for more smoothies.

for example, English grandmothers were invited to knit 'caps' for smoothie bottles in the winter so the bottles would not catch cold. In total, 230,000 granny hats were made and the £115,000 raised was given to Age Concern, a charity dedicated to the well-being and care of senior citizens. Innocent is the fastest growing beverage company in the UK and is currently at a point in the growth cycle where it will need to manage carefully what can only be described as explosive growth. Above all else, as I discuss in this chapter, the company has succeeded through a combination of differentiation, authenticity, innovation and social idealism. In each of these ways, Innocent is, even in its relative youth and small size, a prototypical HCE. In everything it does, from the way it incorporates user-centred feedback in the development of its products, to its human-centred and democratic employee policies, Innocent is successful because it is different. Innocent has the courage to innovate and the market success to prove it.

9.2   Should We Quit Our Jobs?

The story of Innocent Drinks is a textbook case of user-centred design and innovation. The company's three founders - Adam Balon, Jon Wright and Richard Reed - were close friends at university, where they often talked about building a business together. From there they each ventured into respectable professional work, Reed in advertising and Balon and Wright in management consulting. Their entrepreneurial aspirations and conversations continued alongside their various careers until, in 1998, they decided to actually try something.

Somewhat randomly, they landed on the idea of making healthy fruit drinks. For six months in 1998, they spent £500 on fruit, experimenting with various combinations and coming up with several smoothie recipes that they thought were pretty good. Knowing that their product was not only quickly perishable but also very expensive (at £2/bottle), they started their journey with a steep, uphill climb. Their mantra at this stage was 'build something pure and simple, and people will come'. This is a similar approach to that cited earlier by Google's Marissa Mayer, who says 'give people something simple and easy to love, and the money will follow'. With an entirely different type of product and experience, the Innocent approach shares many basic elements with the Google story.

After coming up with what the three felt were winning recipes, they set up a stall at a small music festival in London late in 1998. In a BBC interview, Reed describes how they went about that now legendary event. 'We put up a big sign saying, "Do you think we should give up our jobs to make these smoothies?" And put out a bin saying "Yes" and a bin saying "No", and asked people to put the empty bottles in the right bin. At the end of the weekend the "Yes" bin was full so we went in the next day and resigned.'

At this point they had no funding to scale up the business and nothing in the way of a real business plan. After writing to friends and family seeking investors, they got lucky when Maurice Pinto, an American investor, loaned them £250,000 to start the business. The rest, as they say, is history… but not really. The process by which they took that initial investment and turned themselves into the fastest growing drinks company in the UK, with 183 employees, 65 per cent of the UK smoothie market, offices in London, Manchester, Dublin, Paris, Amsterdam and Copenhagen and revenue of £120m, is in fact a short but highly instructive lesson in innovation. The way they have grown the company, through its employee-centric, customer-centric and socially idealistic management agenda, makes it a textbook example of an HCE.

A core set of creative managerial principles and practices, as well as the overarching ecological and social perspective that they share, has provided Innocent with a distinct cultural identity.

From the beginning, Innocent was strapped for cash and, perhaps more dauntingly, for industry-specific knowledge and expertise. Reed's experience in advertising was helpful, to be sure. But growing a business in the food and drinks industry was new to them all. A core set of creative managerial principles and practices, as well as the overarching ecological and social perspective that they share, has provided Innocent with a distinct cultural identity that both motivates employees to be a part of something important *and* draws in customers who want to be a part of those values as well.

9.3   Drucker's Innocence

If the purpose of a business is, as Peter Drucker suggests, to 'create a customer', then Innocent has been a story right out of the pages of a Drucker text. In the late 1990s, when Innocent first offered its products to the market, consumers were becoming increasingly conscious of, and sensitive to, what they were eating, where it was sourced and what the implications and impacts of that sourcing were. Companies such as Whole Foods in the US also benefited from this rising tide of food awareness, much as Innocent has in the UK. The idealism of the offer and the brand was simple yet powerful: to make something that was absolutely 100 per cent natural and pure - just fruits and their juices. The basic idea was to make something that made people 'a bit healthier each day'. Critics might see such statements as only Marketing 101, but the company maintains it is sincere in its goal of making people healthier and the world a better place. Innocent constantly seeks and takes seriously feedback from customers, tweaking recipes according to the feedback and even creating new formulas recommended by customers. A recent Design Council case study of the company states: 'few companies embrace their customers' views, opinions, thoughts and ideas as wholeheartedly as

Innocent Drinks, which, right from the very outset, has relied on customer feedback and engagement to drive its products, brand values and strategic direction'.

It is the culture of the company and the values it embodies that connect its customers to it. Part of this is the external, public face that the company presents in terms of the Innocent Foundation. The company directs 10 per cent of its profit to the foundation, which spends money to help people in the countries where it sources much of its fruit. This sort of 'giving back' resonates with Innocent's customers and this creates part of the customer loyalty and brand equity that the company now enjoys.

In addition, and importantly for my discussion here, there is the virtuous spiral at Innocent which begins with the way the company relates to, respects and manages its employees. At Innocent's cultural core is a commitment to a creative, employee-led approach to solving problems and to coming up with new ways of doing things and bringing new products to market. On the one hand, it includes integrating customer comments and tastes into the way it generates new smoothies and other drinks. On the other hand, in the way it operates internally - i.e. in terms of the way it manages its people - it is a prototypical HCE.

Consistently ranked as one of the 'best places to work in the UK', Innocent has a loyal and committed staff. This is due, in large part, to the tangible commitments that it makes to its employees. These are not platitudes or shibboleths such as 'our people are our most important asset'; rather, they are real policy commitments and resource allocations that employees actually experience and can count on. Specifically, this manifests itself in the way important decisions at the company are made. Just as at Google, there are many people who want to work for Innocent, so competition for vacancies is intense. As

It is the culture of the company and the values it embodies that connect its customers to it.

In the way Innocent operates internally - i.e. in terms of the way it manages its people - it is a prototypical HCE.

a result, the company has its pick of talent. Once in the company, though, the freedom that employees experience reflects a high level of trust.

A combination of high levels of talent plus high levels of freedom at work is the formula by which the culture of the company is being built. The Design Council case study describes Innocent's culture in the following way: 'The company has developed an internal creative culture which it has managed to sustain despite an extended period of development, both in the UK and Europe. Skilful recruitment and effective communication lie at the heart of the company's cultural development, ensuring creative involvement from every department and a company wide commitment to success'. Dan Germain, Innocent's Head of Creative, puts it in these terms: 'We invest lots of time finding smart people to come and work at Innocent… Smart people are creative, driven, funny, friendly and focused. Without great people, Innocent would not be here today.'

It is easy to poke fun at comments like these, as they appear to be recycled 'employees-first' slogans. However, there is something qualitatively different about the way Innocent goes about just about everything. Insisting on this, Germain says that the company's valuing of creativity goes beyond just the typical areas of design, style and communication. Creativity is 'just as pronounced in the way that we come up with new ideas for drinks, or in our operations and logistics teams - they're the ones who have to solve incredibly complex problems at just a moment's notice'. Open communication and debates about what constitutes effective creativity drive the company's distinctly *open* culture: 'If people aren't involved in all decisions, big and small, then they start to feel unloved and removed from the business and its success. So we get together as a company as much as possible, so that people can share their thoughts and ideas.' There are quarterly

> A combination of high levels of talent plus high levels of freedom at work is the formula by which the culture of the company is being built.

> Open communication and debates about what constitutes effective creativity drive the company's distinctly *open* culture.

meetings, monthly forums for debates and weekly 'catch-up' meetings for the whole company. Clearly, as the company grows there will eventually be too many people for these meetings to be managed easily. Right now, though, these types of meetings and gatherings help define the company's culture. As Germain puts it, 'these all help democratize the idea generation process at the company'. Recall earlier conversations about Southwest Air, Google and BMW, where employees in different departments throughout the company are encouraged to generate fresh ideas that can be driven across the organization.

Commenting directly on the power of its culture in driving its business, Germain summarizes these themes, saying that, 'Without great ideas to improve the business, we wouldn't exist as a company. So I'd say that creative culture is worth about £65 million to us'. A couple of important points are being made (or reiterated) here. First is the direct link that Germain makes between the company's open culture and its financial success. Second is the sheer scope and speed of that financial success. The company's revenue for 2006 was around £80m, which, for a firm founded in 1998, is remarkable. At the time of writing, Innocent's year-end revenue for 2007 is projected at £120m, which indicates that the company's growth is staggering. Managing such growth will inevitably be one of the young company's biggest challenges over the next few years.

9.4   The Cause

Connecting its internal, creative corporate culture with the external brand expectation that Innocent has built up will help Innocent to manage its growth. One company motto states that 'with a non-corporate attitude, a sincere commitment to the cause, and creative thinking, it is possible to create a fast growing company that acts responsibly'. But just what is this 'cause'?

An important dimension of Innocent's resonance with its customers *and* employees is something that it shares with companies such as Whole Foods, Ben & Jerry's, Google and the Body Shop: a certain form of idealism. As Richard Reed put it in the BBC interview, 'there's a touch of hippy in us'. What does this mean, though, for the business? First, and most importantly, it refers to the social idealism I have been talking about here, which sits at the centre of the company's identity: 'Simplicity, purity and innocence'. And health. Innocent's idealism unites its employees and their values with the aspirations of a healthier and more sustainable life also held by their customers. This is part of a larger, generational shift that Jim Collins pointed to earlier, one that continues to define the Innocent brand and the experience of its products.

In a recent *Financial Times* article, Adam Nicolson interviews the writer Barbara Kingsolver about her decision to pursue a lifestyle where she and her family 'live off the land' in rural Virginia, grow much of their own food and source much of the rest of their food locally. The emphasis on local sourcing, often of organic food, is part of a growing movement (in the UK and the US) that is akin to the 'slow food' movement that thrives in places such as Northern California, southwest Britain, Oregon and most of France. The slow food or 'buy local and organic' movement is clearly a reaction to what is perceived by many as a destructive turn away from natural lifestyles. Critics of people like Kingsolver accuse her of fabricating a sense of panic or desperation, suggesting that the crisis exists only in the minds and lives of relatively affluent Westerners who can 'go back to Arcadia' in this sort of way. For Kingsolver, there is a legitimate reason to feel desperate. 'It is normal for an animal to have a feeling of panic when we realize we have done something stupid.

Do you realize this is the first generation of children in the US with a shorter life expectancy than their parents? And why is that? Because we have been feeding them the wrong things, coming down an industrial food pipeline, actually reducing their prospects for life.'

I am not suggesting that by drinking Innocent smoothies you can or will increase your life expectancy. Rather, what makes Innocent a powerful (and perhaps even important) business and brand is what it represents. For the company, and for its customers, it represents *doing* something. It represents 'taking charge' and a refusal to accept that what is generically offered up as food is good enough. It represents, in short, a kind of lifestyle activism, expressed through a consumer brand. In the UK, in particular, Innocent Drinks currently provides a clear consumer space and choice for this type of consumer idealism.

What makes Innocent a powerful business and brand is what it represents. For the company, and for its customers, it represents *doing* something.

9.5   Fruitstock

Innocent tries to hold up its side of the equation when each year in August it hosts a music festival, Fruitstock, in London's Regent Park. The event includes live bands, yoga sessions, massages, bouquet making and a carousel and farmyard for children. Each year it raises thousands of pounds for the charity Well Child. Well Child is a not-for-profit organization focused on providing financial resources to children with chronic diseases. While Fruitstock may seem like pure marketing in some respects, it is an opportunity to showcase its values and raise money for one of its favourite charities. The name of the event - Fruitstock - shows the 'bit of hippy' that Richard Reed mentioned earlier.

Of course no corporate story is free of controversy, as the online postings by Whole Foods' John Mackey demonstrate. Innocent's decision to sell smoothies at

McDonald's has attracted considerable negative publicity. So far, the company is sticking with its decision to sell to McDonald's, saying that their smoothies are healthier than the sucrose-laden drinks generally for sale at McDonald's and therefore they are simply offering consumers a healthier choice. Time will tell as to how this affects, if at all, the Innocent brand.

Like Southwest Airlines in the low cost travel business, Whole Foods in the natural grocery business, Starbucks in the café and media businesses and Google in the Internet search business, Innocent is a category-defining innovator in the British (and European) drinks industry. It *is* the smoothie market in the UK. Of course there are competitors in the market, not the least of which are the own brands offered by major grocery chains such as Tesco, Sainsbury's, Asda and Marks & Spencer. But in ways that are important to its customers, Innocent occupies a cultural space different from those occupied by these other companies. Innocent's commitment to being different (both within the company and within its market place) suggests that for the time being its 'pattern languages' have created a virtuous spiral organization whose future looks very bright.

10 'Designed in China' by Shanghai Tang

10.1 To Return to Innovation by Design

My final case study brings the conversation full circle. Early on in the book I cited the work of *Business Week*'s Bruce Nussbaum, one of the world's leading voices chronicling the growing heft of design-focused innovation in the world of business. Even as recently as two years ago, Nussbaum and others were writing about the importance of design in Western business as part of the challenge of 'moving up the global value chain' (towards design) in an increasingly flat global business world. The logic in this argument, while reasonable and well articulated, may eventually prove to be short-lived as it relates to China.

The idea is that as cheap manufacturing in Asia makes Western manufacturing expensive and unprofitable, the competitive advantage for Western firms comes to reside in *designing* the (world's) products, which are then made in economies with lower costs for labour and materials. This remains true. However, China, in particular, is quickly becoming a centre of design in its own right and the world's consumers are beginning to witness a shift from 'made in China' to 'designed in China'. While still a large manufacturing base to be sure, China is also rapidly moving up the global value chain towards the top end of design. From cars to computers to clothes, China is turning out global brands for sale throughout the world. One such brand, Shanghai Tang, aspires to be the first upscale Chinese luxury brand available in capital cities worldwide. As shoppers in London, Paris, Hong Kong, New York, Dubai, Milan *and* Shanghai become loyal

The world's consumers are beginning to witness a shift from 'made in China' to 'designed in China'.

customers at Shanghai Tang, the design-led innovation story comes full circle.

10.2 Designed in China

Founded in 1994 by Hong Kong entrepreneur David Tang, Shanghai Tang's current growth and global splash is closely tied to the story of China itself. As China's smog and pollution demonstrate, it is going through its own latter-day Industrial Revolution. Its difficult relationship with the International Olympic Committee regarding its air quality is a constant reminder of this. At the same time, though, a creative revolution is occurring in China, which coexists with its rapid industrialization. Government policy makers and business leaders know that the future of Chinese competitiveness lies in its creative industries - design, architecture, advertising, music, entertainment, fashion, film - as much as it does in heavy industry.

For example, a recent *Business Week* article suggests that there are already 400 design schools in China, cranking out 10,000 design graduates every year. With government backing in place for most of these schools, it is obvious that Design with a capital 'D' is a priority for the government. The cover article in the June 2007 issue of *Fast Company* chronicles the design revolution that is under way in China. Innovation in music, gaming, films and architecture is becoming a staple item on China's business and cultural agenda. While some of this can be seen as a hurried face lift in advance of the 2008 Summer Olympics, some of the innovation is already maturing and being successfully exported around the world.

Shanghai Tang originally aspired to bring the 1930s 'Shanghai glamour look', (representing an era when Shanghai was referred to as the 'Paris of the East') to haute couture fashion design. To incorporate elements of traditional Chinese culture into wearable, contemporary clothes was the founding concept behind the company. The company has stumbled a couple of times over the past thirteen years, but it currently seems to be riding the China tide and is now in a high-growth mode. Today the company is a global 'cultural innovator', one of the first Chinese firms to distil what economist Joseph Nye describes as 'soft power'. Nye defines soft power as the combination of Chinese 'economic cachet with its cultural cachet', which drives 'brand China' throughout the world.

In Early 2008, Shanghai Tang had 30 stores around the world. In 1998, the Swiss luxury goods company, Richemont, bought a majority stake in the company from David Tang. It is still a privately held company and the current CEO, Raphaël le Masne de Chermont, is close-mouthed about the company's sales figures. However, he and others close to the company will say that the business grew by almost 40 per cent in 2006 and was profitable in every market except the US. Indeed, it has struggled in the US for many years. It had a horrible experience with its New York store in 1999, where it was forced to shut down a Madison Avenue location after only 20 months, but the company has used that experience (or iteration) as a cautionary tale for its current global expansion.

Known for its qipaos, the traditional, thin-cut Chinese dresses, Shanghai Tang now designs all sorts of clothing and accessories for women, men and children. It aspires to be a global luxury brand spoken in the same breath as Armani, Gucci, Versace and Yves St. Laurent. The driving force behind its resurgence and current global growth has been its particular approach to innovation. David Tang is quick to disavow descriptors of Shanghai Tang as 'where East meets West', which he says degrades the brand. To avoid this sort of brand debasement, the company has learned to take seriously its 'Chineseness'

> To avoid brand debasement, the company has learned to take seriously its 'Chineseness' and its obligation to represent that identity faithfully in its designs.

and its obligation to represent that identity faithfully in its designs. Two years after its famous Madison Avenue meltdown, Chermont met up with Joanne Ooi, an American of Chinese descent who was living in Hong Kong, and this relationship crystallized and defined the company's growth path. When Ooi and Chermont met, she was designing her own ready to wear qipaos in an effort to, in her words, 'eat Shanghai Tang for lunch'.

Chermont was introduced to Ooi through a headhunter and the relationship that they established has been pivotal for the company. Chermont invited Ooi to have a walk through the flagship store in Hong Kong and to write up her thoughts and impressions of what she saw. Her response was brutal and straightforward: 'It is an overpriced Chinese emporium that has no credibility with local Chinese people, let alone with fashion people. Its very narrow market is high-end tourists. It's a once-in-a-lifetime destination shopping experience, a kind of fashion Disneyland. Plus, it's unwearable and eccentric.' Chermont responded to her stinging criticism by offering her a job as Creative Director and head of marketing. Ooi recalls that when she took the job the brand had 'no depth, no sincerity, no differentiation'. This would be her mandate: to bring cultural authenticity and meaningful differentiation to the brand.

10.3   The Anthropology of Innovation at Shanghai Tang

What makes the Shanghai Tang story so intriguing within the present discussion is its distinct and culturally rich approach to innovation. When Ooi came into the fold of the business, she and Chermont found common ground in what *Fast Company* magazine refers to as 'the primary imperative of the fashion industry: constant innovation'. In the case of Shanghai Tang, its approach to innovation

Shanghai Tang's approach to innovation could be called *culture-centred* as much as human-centred, in that the focus of its design strategy is on understanding and translating (into final designs) various elements of Chinese history, culture and style.

Ooi's immersion into Chinese culture, language and daily life is similar to the ideal field experience of a cultural anthropologist.

could be called *culture-centred* as much as human-centred, in that the focus of its design strategy is on understanding and translating (into final designs) various elements of Chinese history, culture and style. While in some respects this has been the intent of the company since its inception, in Ooi's view the company was wavering on this commitment when she signed on.

Ooi's arrival at Shanghai Tang has been fortuitous for both her and the company. When she arrived in Hong Kong in the early 1990s with a law degree from the University of Pennsylvania, her initial plan was to practise corporate law in the city. She did not connect with the culture of corporate law at the time, but she fell in love with Hong Kong and with Chinese culture. She says she was mesmerized by the place, the people and the culture of the city. An American of Chinese descent, she quickly felt at home in the city and set out straight away to learn Mandarin and to study Chinese history. In a curious way, Ooi's immersion into Chinese culture, language and daily life is similar to the ideal field experience of a cultural anthropologist. Her connection to the place, via her family background, has given her enough of an insider's status to fit in; but, as an outsider, she is also driven to learn, introduce and apply new things. This combination has bred in her a passion for capturing a Chinese cultural authenticity that she can then embed within her design work at Shanghai Tang. Her commitment to this cultural authenticity has helped her and the company to reinvigorate the brand completely.

For Ooi, each collection she puts together is a project unto itself. First, she conducts research into various elements of Chinese history and culture and comes up with an organizing theme. The collection becomes a reflection of that theme. She is clear about her intention: 'I decided that it was really, really imperative to create cultural roots for every single product'. She then shares the various ingredients she wants to pull together with the 16 other designers and consultants from around the world who help her in the design process and slowly a 'look' begins to emerge. The fall/winter 2003 collection, for example, was inspired by the traditional costumes of the Miao, a little-known ethnic group in China. This was the first of her research-grounded collections. It was such a hit that it has become Shanghai Tang's core design strategy.

Today Ooi travels extensively throughout China, going to antiques markets, art galleries, museums and as many historic sites as she can. She takes notes, makes drawings, sketches, takes pictures and otherwise carries on like an anthropologist in the field. Like an anthropologist talking of her relationship with her field notes, Ooi says: 'If I lost my notebook, I would be lobotomized'.

Shanghai Tang's design strategy underscores the intense connection between culture and cultural understanding on the one hand and customer-focused innovation on the other. In this respect, Shanghai Tang has developed a finely tuned system of culture-centred innovation, a system (and organization) that is different from the other HCE approaches discussed in the book. Ooi's ambition, that Shanghai Tang's designs be relevant and meaningful for *Chinese* consumers, makes an important point. Like ethnographic researchers at other companies discussed in this book, Ooi has focused the company's research on the cultural well-spring - Chinese history, culture and pop-culture - to which Chinese consumers are connected as part of their day-to-day lives. This, then, is the litmus test for Ooi. If its products are not authentic and meaningful for *Chinese* consumers, then the company is not succeeding. That Shanghai Tang is an upmarket luxury brand might make this seem irrelevant, at least for the millions of Chinese consumers who could never afford to shop at the stores. However, the rapidly growing middle and upper classes in China are no less Chinese that

Shanghai Tang's design strategy underscores the intense connection between culture and cultural understanding on the one hand and customer-focused innovation on the other.

Connecting (or not) with Chinese consumers is the 'authenticity reality check' that Ooi wants.

their compatriots and connecting (or not) with Chinese consumers is the 'authenticity reality check' that Ooi wants. In turn, it is this 'culture-centredness' and cultural authenticity that make the brand alluring and desirable in other capital cities.

As much as any other Chinese brand at the present time, Shanghai Tang embodies the 'soft power' that Joseph Nye talks about. Soft power exists in the consumer market space and in the imagination of consumers around the world. That is, Shanghai Tang's embodiment of China's aesthetics and cultural potential exists externally, in the market. At the same time, *within* the company itself in its day-to-day operations, the company also commits to innovation and to exploring new and 'better' ways of operating. The company's former Chief Financial Officer, Simon Drakeford, reflects on how flexible the company was when he first arrived and identified critical changes that needed to be made. When he joined the company, it was profitable and growing, but bloated. Account reports, he says, were longer than a 'CIA intelligence study' and difficult to understand. Committed to the notion of full financial disclosure to all employees, similar to the approach taken by John Mackey at Whole Foods, he took steps to ensure that all employees had all the information that they needed or wanted. 'The free flow of financial information within all levels of the organization, Drakeford believes, is crucial to a company's success. If employees understand the company's financial goals, he says, then they'll understand how to get there'.

'If employees understand the company's financial goals...then they'll understand how to get there.'

With the sort of openness of information within the company that Drakeford talks about, combined with the company's efforts at connecting 'outwardly' with the cultural roots that drive its design strategy, Shanghai Tang is adeptly aligning its internal management processes with its external brand identity in a winning formula.

The company's success as a culture-centred enterprise is an instructive example for firms in developing markets looking to leverage their cultural identities into global brands.

Authenticity builds trust, transparency and, in the end, sustainability.

Its timing could not be better. The 'China story' shows few signs of slowing down or diminishing as a force in the global economy and, as a result of this, Shanghai Tang is in a *sweet spot* of sorts. As an ambassador for China's 'soft power', the company's success as a culture-centred enterprise is an instructive example for firms in developing markets looking to leverage their cultural identities into global brands. The unifying word here is *authenticity*. We've seen this as it relates to the managerial styles and values at the other HCEs discussed here and it is a critical ingredient in Shanghai Tang's success as well. The 'real thing' cannot be faked, whether that thing is management communication or fashion design. Authenticity builds trust, transparency and, in the end, sustainability.

11 Innovating in a Theory X World

11.1 X and Y Views

In Section 7.8 I briefly outlined Douglas McGregor's distinction between what he referred to as Theory X and Theory Y views of people and work. He suggests that these two perspectives are for the most part opposing views of the world. Theory X assumes that most employees (people) dislike work, can generally *not* be trusted and must be motivated and coerced with carrots and sticks. Theory Y, on the other hand, proposes that work is a natural human capacity and that people *do* like work and can find it intrinsically motivating. Theory X is McGregor's term for describing what I have been describing here as *traditionalism*, while Theory Y is his way of describing a more decentralized, hands-off approach to management. He suggests three core assumptions (about human nature and human behaviour) that define a Theory X view of the world:

1. *'The average human being has an inherent dislike of work and will avoid it if he can.'* Regarding this initial assumption, McGregor makes an interesting and perhaps somewhat provocative follow-up point. He goes on to suggest that this assumption has deep roots. 'The punishment of Adam and Eve for eating the fruit in the Tree of Knowledge was to be banned from Eden into a world where they had to work for a living. The stress that management places on productivity, on the concept of a "fair day's work", on the evils of featherbedding and restriction of output... reflect an underlying belief that management

must counteract an inherent human tendency to avoid work'.

2. *'Because of this inherent dislike for work, humans must be coerced, controlled, directed and threatened with punishment to do the jobs they are asked (or told) to do.'* Common criticisms of companies that allow 'democracy à la Hippy Capitalism' say that they may be cool and fun, but 'that isn't real business'. As I have been eager to show here, this sort of traditional 'common sense' may be common but it doesn't necessarily make much sense.

3. *'The average human being prefers to be directed, wishes to avoid responsibility, has relatively little ambition, and wants security above all.'* This third point directly contradicts Jim Collins' earlier comments where he suggests that, given the right context and circumstances, work can be a place where one can find 'sanctuary and meaning'. It would seem that defining the context and circumstances of work, in order to get the most natural and discretionary energy out of employees, has become one of the most important responsibilities among managers working in the New Pragmatism.

By contrast, the core assumptions within a Theory Y view of the world, according to McGregor, are essentially the opposite of Theory X and can be easily recognized in the psychological employment contracts of the seven firms discussed here. Psychological contracts consist of the emotional and behavioural expectations and tradeoffs between employers and employees. Some of the behavioural assumptions that, according to McGregor, characterize Theory Y resonate loudly with how I am

Psychological contracts consist of the emotional and behavioural expectations and tradeoffs between employers and employees.

defining 'innovative cultures'. McGregor outlines these in the following way:

1. The expenditure of physical and mental effort is as natural as play and rest.

2. External control and the threat of punishment are not the only means for bringing about effort towards organizational objectives.

3. Commitment to objectives is a function of the rewards associated with their achievement.

4. The average human being learns, under proper conditions, not only to accept but to seek responsibility.

5. The capacity to exercise a relatively high degree of imagination, ingenuity and creativity in the solution of organizational problems is widely, not narrowly, distributed in the population.

6. Under the conditions of modern, industrial life, the intellectual potentialities of the average human being are only partially realized.

Even though written over 40 years ago, many of McGregor's generalizations, particularly numbers five and six, are clearly recognizable today in the types of companies I discuss here. When managerial assumptions run counter to the impulses of human nature, against Alexander's 'timeless way', organizations might be highly efficient, for sure, but they are unlikely to be holistic or enjoyable places to work. That is, they become the opposite of the human-centred enterprise. This becomes an important value if one accepts Jim Collins' critical assumption, where he says that 'if your competitive scorecard is money, you will always lose'.

11.2   Leading by Design

It is at this point in the discussion that the early conversation about design, design thinking and the 'design as innovation' methodology becomes helpful. If and when a company chooses to begin the movement towards systemic and sustainable innovation, Roger Martin's earlier admonition to companies to learn how to think like 'design shops' is one particular way to take action. This entails evolving a particular way of dealing with constraints, a general commitment to abductive thinking, experimentation and a commitment to developing an ethnographic understanding of what's going on in the consumer spaces and employee spaces around them.

More than anything else, design and 'design thinking' refer to a certain view of the world. In their book, *Managing as Designing*, Richard Boland and Fred Collopy (of Case Western Reserve University's Weatherhead School of Management) refer to this view as a *design attitude* and contrast it with the worldview of traditional managers and MBAs, which they refer to as the *decision attitude*. By focusing on the idea that decision-making can be turned into a 'science' (as adherents of the field known as Decision Science would suggest), a whole range of assumptions about what is and what is not knowable and doable are made. According to the logic of the decision attitude, once all the data surrounding a given problem have been gathered and all the potential alternative courses of action are known and are factored out, the correct and best course of action can be taken. The problem with this, of course, as Herbert Simon indicated in the 1960s, is that our rationality (as well as the 'data' that inform it) is inherently finite and bounded.

There is an important congruity between McGregor's argument and the one made by Collopy and Boland.

A Theory X view of the world conforms to Collopy and Boland's notion of the *decision attitude*, while the Theory Y perspective is similar to Collopy and Boland's idea of the *design attitude*. Within a Theory X/Decision framework, managers work at gathering all of the necessary data relevant to a problem, sort through all possible alternatives and make the 'right decision'. That decision is then announced to all of the 'little people', whose job is to then go out and execute. No questions asked: just execute. A Theory Y/Design framework, by contrast, holds that there are likely to be numerous viable solutions to a given problem and that the actual users and the employees closest to the consumer interface will probably have meaningful input into the strategy-building process itself. A design attitude elevates the daily work of employees beyond mere execution and enables them to participate in the crafting and implementation of innovation strategies.

According to Collopy and Boland, this requires a vision of the manager or leader as someone capable of *giving form* to new things. This echoes what I have been saying here about the differences between 'managing the known' and 'building the unknown':

> There is something tragically missing from management practice and education today, and missing from our management icons. That missing element is an image of the manager as an idea generator who gives form to new possibilities with a well developed vocabulary of design. Managers as form-givers care deeply about the world that is being shaped by a business and refuse to accept the default alternatives. They understand that the design of better products, processes, and services is their

A Theory Y/Design framework holds that there are likely to be numerous viable solutions to a given problem and that the actual users and the employees closest to the consumer interface will probably have meaningful input into the strategy-building process itself.

core responsibility. The design attitude is the source of those inventions. A decision does not generate inventions, no matter how advanced its analytic capabilities.

'Engineering, medicine, business, architecture, and painting are concerned not with the necessary but with the contingent - not how things are but how they might be - in short, with design'.

Or, to use Herbert Simon's phrasing of the same form-giving dynamic: 'Engineering, medicine, business, architecture, and painting are concerned not with the necessary but with the contingent - not how things are but how they might be - in short, with design'. Infusing an organization with 'design thinking as an innovation methodology' is, of course, easier said than done. However, not only can this deepen your innovative capabilities and increase your innovation hit rate, but it can also help build a more engaging work environment where employees *want* to be and to which they *want* to contribute.

11.3 An Innovative Culture is an Engaged Culture

Design is always for someone else, not for the designer, so it is important to learn how to put oneself in another person's shoes as a central step in the design process.

IDEO Chief Executive, Tim Brown, talks often about the importance of *empathy* in the design process. Empathy is the unifying principle that lies at the heart of building human-centred enterprises. As Brown says, design is always for someone else, not for the designer, so it is important to learn how to put oneself in another person's shoes as a central step in the design process. Hopefully I have demonstrated here that it is possible to build a profitable enterprise that is also a human-centred enterprise. In practice, making the journey from being a traditional firm that is focused on a 'decision attitude', on a fear of constraints, on execution and on quarterly pressures to becoming an innovative, outward-looking, empathetic and design-focused firm is challenging on several fronts.

From a customer's perspective there is only a product, service or experience that is or is not desirable.

First, there is a need for organizations, beginning with their leadership and top management, to learn to think beyond the functional silos that make up the departmental structure of businesses as well as business school curricula. From a customer's perspective, there is no such thing as Research and Development (R&D), HR, Marketing, Finance or Operations - there is only a product, service or experience that is or is not desirable. Functional/ silo thinking is one of the most problematic constraints to building HCEs. Roger Martin and his colleagues at Rotman have been working brilliantly over the past several years to build 'integrative curricula' that bring together and apply different modes of thinking to problem solving and innovation challenges. Rotman's partnership with the Ontario College of Art & Design is a prime example of this type of integrative curriculum. More specifically within the goal of developing integrative thinking across disciplines, HCEs depend on integration between Sales and Marketing on the one hand and between HRM and Operations on the other. Even using these traditional labels is distracting, as it is the process of giving labels to certain activities that implicitly legitimizes them and makes them 'real'. Perhaps the idea is better framed in terms of questions: How can the experience of customers and the experience of employees be brought into the same managerial frame? How can the work of people in HR be tied directly to the needs, aspirations and experiences of the company's customers? What would the work of an HR staff member look like in a company where this integrative type of thinking was predominant? Would it change? If so, how?

These are, at this point in time, almost unanswerable questions. Most businesses could not satisfactorily answer them and nor could business school faculties intelligently address them. Having taught in business schools for many years, I can say that we (my colleagues and I) are more a

With very few exceptions, business schools do little to encourage and build an alternative approach to management practice.

part of the problem than we are part of the solution. We endorse and support the very type of thinking and teaching that produces MBAs, a decision attitude, traditional firms, a shareholder value ideology, functional careers, sameness, assumptions about knowability, execution and high levels of employee turnover and public cynicism. With very few exceptions, business schools do little to encourage and build an alternative approach to management practice, one that might see as normal things such as invention, design attitude, innovative cultures, sustainable competitive value, integrative careers, differentiation, the unknown, creation, employee retention and public support. Framed as a series of contrasts, similar to the one presented earlier by Roger Martin, these differences look something like this:

TRADITIONAL ENTERPRISE	HUMAN-CENTRED ENTERPRISE
Mathematics/Economics/ Psychology	Architecture/Design/ Anthropology
Theory X	Theory Y
MBAs	MBDs
Decision Attitude	Design Attitude
Functional Careers	Integrative Careers
Sameness	Differentiation
Recipes	Solving Wicked Problems
'Already Known Results'	Iterative Processes
Order-Giving	Form-Giving
Execution	Invention
MANAGING THE KNOWN	BUILDING THE UNKNOWN

In practice, of course, few firms exist at either extreme in this sort of dichotomy, but the oppositions are instructive nonetheless. Budget-constrained managers of public firms will say, predictably, that this 'creative and integrative thinking' is all well and good but, 'Hey, I'm trying to run a

There *are* identifiable steps that can be incorporated into a given set of corporate practices that can jumpstart the journey to design, innovation and a human-centred agenda.

business here!' This is the ultimate cop-out and is actually saying, 'Look, neither I nor my organization have the courage to try anything new, and if we do, we'll be fired anyway!' The challenge in moving forward is twofold. First there is the step of admitting, in the mirror, that the firm in question is in fact grounded on the left side of this continuum: on the side of fear, Theory X assumptions, control as an end unto itself, etc. As they say in therapy, the first step is to admit that there is a problem. The second aspect of this equation is more straightforward. While not simple, there *are* identifiable steps, indeed a methodological process, that can be incorporated into a given set of corporate practices that can jumpstart the journey to design, innovation and a human-centred agenda.

11.4 A Methodology for Building HCEs

There are four steps or activities that can be put in place to move an organization from the Theory X/Decision Attitude side of the continuum towards the adaptive, Theory Y/Design Attitude side.

There are four steps or activities that can be put in place to move an organization from the Theory X/Decision Attitude side of the continuum towards the adaptive, Theory Y/Design Attitude side: 1) Use ethnographic observation across the firm; 2) Reward internal process innovations from the bottom up; 3) Involve customers in everything and 4) Externalize leadership development and tie it to customer experience.

While each of these activities does require time and money, they are relatively cheap compared with the massive amounts of wasted energy, lost productivity and costs associated with employee attrition that are endemic in many organizations in most sectors of the economy.

1. *Ethnographic observation.* A simple starting point towards building integrative thinking and practice throughout an organization begins with the incorporation of systematic observation

of relevant human behaviour in its naturally occurring context. This applies to both consumer experiences and behaviour and to employee experiences and behaviour equally. Not surveys. Not questionnaires. Not focus groups. But watching, interacting with, filming, drawing and participating in the daily activities of a particular group of people. Eventually, participants forget or bracket off the presence of the researcher and his/her equipment and natural behaviours reappear. Leading ethnographic research consultancies have refined the in-context research process both with customers of large firms and their employees. Incorporating ethnographic research can begin to build bridges between customers and employees in such a way that the notion of 'integrative thinking' can become more than just provocative words. Unlike the more commonly used psychological approaches (surveys, profiles, etc.) to understanding employees and customers, the ethnographic sensibility exists at the intersection of micro and macro levels of meaning, aspiration and motivation. Larger and more broadly shared cultural assumptions and aspirations unite the experiences of consumers and employees in ways that the Mathematics/Economics/Psychology model simply does not capture. An empathetic look across the (artificial) boundaries that isolate various constituents in the corporate landscape can be a helpful lens through which one can better understand patterns and trends, and thus become more adept at thinking in abductive and innovative frames.

2. *Reward internal process innovations from the bottom up.* If, in the search to improve understanding of the unarticulated goals and

> Incorporating ethnographic research can begin to build bridges between customers and employees in such a way that the notion of 'integrative thinking' can become more than just provocative words.

aspirations of consumers, companies can find competitive advantage in the generation of new products and services, then why shouldn't the principle of 'user-generated innovation' be applied to a company's own employees? No one knows better than an employee where wasted energy, misspent time and process inefficiencies exist. Rarely, though, do firms show the courage to say, essentially: 'How do you think we should accomplish this, or that?'. Rather, senior managers hold a meeting (with other senior managers) and decide how a certain set of activities are to be done. They announce these activities to 'the little people', who are then measured by how well they meet those targets. Consider the example of Semco, where Chairman, Ricardo Semler, got all of his people together and turned over all such decisions to them. In what configuration should our teams be organized? At what time of day should this manufacturing work be done, say, so that we can all spend less time in traffic? How much time do you actually have to spend at the office to do your work (and therefore how much office space do you actually need)? What can realistically be done from home? In his book, *The Seven Day Weekend*, Semler chronicles how he systematically 'let go' of all such decisions and how the company has grown at around 27.5 per cent a year over the past 14 years. From the time he inherited the company from his father over twenty years ago, Semco has more than quadrupled in size in terms of revenues and profits. Semco is another example of a highly profitable HCE, one that has taken the social experiment of the democratic firm to stratospheric levels of participative management

(Theory Y on steroids) and profitability. That is, Semco invites and strongly encourages employees to devise and design their own work processes as much as they possibly can for themselves and for the profitability of the company. The choices are theirs.

3. *Involve customers in everything.* If, as the study by Stanton Marris suggests, only about five per cent of employee activities in an average firm add value to the end-user, what can be done to improve this situation? Consider the design-innovation process used by IDEO, where they literally and physically include customers/end users in the brainstorming, prototyping and refining phases of their innovation work for clients. This may not be possible in companies across different sectors, but the ideal and principles are applicable. How does this meeting serve the end user? Are we meeting today to tick boxes in our own system, regardless of any inherent value that may come out of it? In the university sector, in schools of business as well as in other kinds of department, faculty members often carry on, like the senior managers at Credit Suisse mentioned earlier, as if we are the end-user. It is difficult-to-impossible to understand, let alone teach, user-centred innovation and Human-Centred Design if we don't know what it is or have never done it. More tangibly, it would seem that incorporating knowledge of a firm's outside environment, including knowledge of changing technologies, customers, competitors, developments abroad, etc, should be made part of performance reviews and performance evaluations. If you don't know where and how your work connects and resonates 'out there' in

If you don't know where and how your work connects and resonates 'out there' hitting all of your internal targets is likely to some extent to be disconnected from user experience.

the broader cultural and economic environment, hitting all of your internal targets might feel good but is likely to some extent to be disconnected from user experience. Internal targets should, by definition, connect to external targets designed to improve customer experience.

4. *Externalize leadership development and tie it to customer experience.* This final point is clearly related to the previous one, but deserves repeating. As the examples of external leadership development activities at Credit Suisse and P&G demonstrate, there are ways of developing talent for innovative firms other than the 'put them on the couch and have them tell you about their relationships with their parents' approach. This is where the Leading by Design approach screams, 'Get off the couch and go do something (meaningful)!' The $20,000 week of self exploration at the Centre for Creative Leadership, where you probe the depths of your unconscious so you can better understand yourself, might be a great piece of personal therapy, but the CCL's own data show that impact on organizational performance for participating firms is extremely difficult to measure. What does a company, much less its customers, have to gain from the psychotherapeutic journeys of people trying to understand why they have made the decisions they have made in life and how they can be better people when they return to the office?

What they need, in fact, is to stop whining, and go shopping! They need to go interact with customers, in a variety of natural contexts on a regular basis. They will learn about themselves as soon as they commit to learning about others. Anthropologists

What does a company, much less its customers, have to gain from the psychotherapeutic journeys of people trying to understand why they have made the decisions they have made in life?

have long known that the best way to learn about yourself is to immerse yourself with others and learn about them first.

In a new field-based and designed-centred leadership development programme, called 'Leading by Design', my colleagues and I at Aquifer Design are trying to invert the traditional paradigm for what constitutes an effective development sequence:

FROM:	TO:
Vision	Doing
Reflection	Creation
Influence	Innovation
Persuasion	Collaboration

Design is both a way of thinking and a specific set of methodologies. It can facilitate the journey from a Theory X traditional corporate mindset, defined and constrained by a decision-attitude, to a Theory Y innovative mindset, defined by a design-attitude. The elemental methodology of design-driven innovation is proven to work. In the end, the point and purpose of a design-centred approach to developing leaders and organizations is a doubling up on *doing*! Close observation of user experience in context, followed by intensive brainstorming, rapid prototyping and interdisciplinary input - and quick iteration that elicits more customer feedback - can and will up your innovation hit rate. The first step in the process, though, is to take the *acid test* and assess where your company sits on the continuum, to determine if you have the courage to make the journey to innovation.

Close observation of user experience in context, followed by intensive brainstorming, rapid prototyping and interdisciplinary input - and quick iteration that elicits more customer feedback - can and will up your innovation hit rate.

Glossary

Abductive Thinking

Roger Martin, Dean of the Rotman School of Management at the University of Toronto, suggests that the most successful innovators incorporate 'abductive thinking' alongside more traditional modes of thinking such as inductive and deductive thinking. Abductive thinking focuses not on what is or what was, but rather on what might be. Abductive thinkers are interested in what sorts of approaches to problem solving have not been tried yet. It is an essential ingredient of design thinking.

Sections 1.6, 5.1, 7.6, 7.9, 11.2, 11.4

Algorithms

An algorithm is a step by step, repeatable formula for solving a given problem. The MBA degree, as taught by most business schools in the world, implies that effective management can be achieved by implementing a managerial 'toolkit'. Particularly, the term algorithm refers to formulas that have been codified into set processess. Some examples of management formulas applied in this way are business process re-engineering (BPR), customer relationship management (CRM) and supply chain management (SCM).

Foreword; Sections 1.6, 3.10, 5.1, 7.11, 8.7

Bobos

Bobos is a French expression used to describe Bourgeois-Bohemians and subsequently popularized in English by journalist David Brooks in his book *Bobos in Paradise*. Brooks parodies late baby boomers in this piece of pop-sociology, where he observes conservative investment bankers eating vegan diets and going on spiritual treks in the Himalayas, while at the same time he finds ageing hippies talking about managing their ever-growing stock portfolios in cafés from Soho to San Francisco. In *Bobos in Paradise*, Brooks describes a consumer landscape where left and right merge into a single vision of bourgeois consumerism.

Sections 6.1, 6.4, 7.6

Consumer Experience Design

In their book, *The Experience Economy: Work is Theater and Every Business a Stage*, Joseph Pine and James Gilmore introduce the notion of the 'experience economy', which is their way of describing the many customer experiences (such as the $4 cup of coffee at Starbucks or Caffe Nero, or an adventure lifestyle at Patagonia) that companies increasingly rely on to sell their brands. Travel, music, food, shopping, expeditions and other consumer categories make up the 'experience economy'. Design firms are hired to help map customer experiences and to enhance customer experience through a practice known as 'experience design'.

Chapter 7; Sections 6.4, 9.2, 0.4, 10.2, 11.4

Customer Experience Immersion

At companies such as P&G and Credit Suisse, a new approach to developing leaders is being adopted. This entails senior managers going into the customer environment and immersing themselves into the daily lives of customers (similar to ethnographic research), where they observe, interview and hang out with customers. At P&G this includes shopping outings, where senior leaders, in conjunction with facilitators from the design firm IDEO, go out and shop for various P&G products in different cultural contexts. These experiences are then used as points of reflection in the leadership development process.

Section 3.5

Cultural Architecture

One way of describing cultural architecture is as the sum total of the commitments that a company makes to its employees. This includes the way companies recruit and develop employees, the amount of freedom and autonomy they are granted and the degree of trust and loyalty that builds up over time. Cultural architecture refers both to policies and physical spaces (i.e. the architecture) in which employees do their work, and the patterns of use that develop and come to define the company.

Sections 2.2, 2.3

d-School

The new Hasso Plattner Institute of Design at Stanford University has quickly become known in design circles as the d-school. The idea of the d-school is presented as a contrast to the shortened version of the Stanford business school, or B-school. Recent articles in the mainstream business press are exploring the increasing number of d-school graduates going to work for large companies looking to increase their innovation success rates.

Sections 3.7, 3.8, 3.10

Design Thinking

According to Herbert Simon, 'design is the transformation of existing conditions into preferred ones' (*Sciences of the Artificial*. Cambridge, MA: MIT Press, 1969, p. 55). Design thinking extends from this basic idea and is a way of imagining and building new things and possibilities. It is grounded in abductive thinking: that is, in a thoughtful consideration of what might be possible. It is also a commitment to a design methodology which follows several key steps: research; brainstorming; prototyping; iteration; user feedback; learning; improvement and implementation. Design thinking has become part of the innovation toolkit for many companies, including Intel, Microsoft, GE and P&G.

Chapter 3; Sections 1.2, 1.6, 2.1, 8.3, 11.2

Disciplines of Innovation

In the emerging landscape of customer-focused innovation, three disciplines have come together to form a new framework and toolkit for generating and sustaining innovation: design and design thinking, ethnography (and anthropological thinking) and architecture. These three disciplines bring together observational research, brainstorming, rapid prototyping, iterative product and service launches and the incorporation of user-feedback into the whole process.

Sections 1.2, 3.2

Drucker's Maxim

Peter Drucker was famous for saying that the purpose of a business was to create a customer and to innovate for that customer. He followed this with the bold assertion that only innovation and marketing produce results and that everything else a business does represents a cost. The current wave of design thinking and innovation led by customer experience is in some ways a re-embrace of this Drucker Maxim.

Sections 1.4, 3.5, 4.6

Ethnography

Ethnography is a research method derived from the academic discipline of anthropology. Used in the corporate environment as a form of consumer culture and consumer behaviour research, it is based on the observation of, and participation, with consumers in the naturally occurring contexts of product use: in homes, offices, shops, hospitals, etc.

Chapter 4; Sections 1.2, 1.3, 1.5, 3.2, 7.6

Experience Architecture

Experience architecture is the sum total of the experience design work done by designers and marketers in creating customer experiences. At Starbucks, for example, this includes detailed attention given to the built environment, the music, the lighting, and all elements of the customer experience.

Section 1.6

Heuristics

Technically, a heuristic is 'a speculative formula', used in the framing and solving of a problem. Used by designers, it refers to the belief that there is rarely a single solution to a given problem, and that an iterative approach (which consistently incorporates user-feedback) to solving problems allows for new and emergent solutions that have yet to be tried. Roger Martin (Dean of the Rotman School of Management at the University of Toronto) suggests that designers' use of heuristics is best understood in contrast to algorithms.

Foreword; Sections 1.6, 3.10, 5.1, 7.11, 8.7

Human-Centred Enterprise

The term 'human-centred enterprise' (HCE) is a reference to firms that focus in equal measure on the user needs and experiences of employees and customers. Companies that are HCEs, to put it simply, 'do well by doing good'. They achieve high levels of growth by creating passionate loyalty among customers while treating employees in openly humanistic ways. Professor Edward Lawler of USC refers to these types of firms (Southwest Airlines, Google, W.L. Gore) as virtuous spiral organizations.

Chapter 2; Sections 1.1, 1.3, 5.4, 5.6, 6.4, 8.7, 9.1, 9.2, 9.3, 10.3, 11.1, 11.3, 11.4

Human-Centred Innovation

Human-centred (or user-centred) innovation is an approach to innovation that is sharply focused on user needs and user experiences, as well as on needs and functions which consumers may not yet have articulated to themselves. It is an approach to innovation borrowed from user-centred design in human-computer interaction design and is supported in corporate innovation efforts by human factors research.

Sections 1.2, 8.1, 9.1, 11.4

Innovation

In his book *The Ten Faces of Innovation*, Tom Kelley defines innovation as 'the creation of value through the implementation of new ideas'. Kelley connects innovation to corporate growth and value creation as part of his attempt to champion the innovation approach used by his employer, IDEO. In a larger, anthropological sense innovation is simply the generation of new solutions to existing problems or the development of new possibilities altogether. Early hominids figuring out how to hunt big game, or harnessing fire for the first time, or the early domestication of plants and animals around 10,000 years ago, would be examples of life-changing innovation. More recently, the Industrial Revolution and the Information Revolution are examples of culture-transforming innovations.

Chapters 1, 3, 4, 8, 10, 11; Sections 6.2, 7.4, 7.6, 7.8, 9.1

Iteration

A mainstay concept in the work of many successful innovators, iteration refers to the understanding that the first version of an idea or product is not necessarily the best or final version. Rather, it is simply the first iteration, or version. An iterative approach to innovation depends on getting user feedback, which is incorporated into subsequent iterations.

Sections 1.3, 1.5, 1.6, 7.6, 8.2, 8.4, 10.2, 11.3, 11.4

Leading as Designing

Corporations (and their leaders) are constantly challenged to generate new ways of working and to develop new products, services and business models in order to differentiate their organizations and make them more competitive. In this respect, whether they think in these terms or not, corporate leaders are doing the work of designers every day. They are constantly trying to transform existing conditions into preferred ones. Leading by Design is an approach to leadership development that makes this explicit, and inserts different elements of design methodology into the leadership development process. The customer immersion processes at Credit Suisse and P&G are early examples of this approach to developing leaders.

Chapter 3; Sections 1.6, 7.9, 8.1, 10.1, 11.2, 11.3, 11.4

Living Organizations

In organizations where the 'timeless way of building' manifests itself, employees are more engaged, content and free to be themselves than in organizations that are built against the grain of human nature. At companies such as SAS Institute, for example, one's home life is seen as more important than one's work life, and as a result the company has extremely low employee turnover and high-levels of employee engagement. Work and work-life are constructed holistically, and this benefits employees as well as the company (The term was pioneered in a slightly different context by writer and organizational thinker Arie de Geus.).

Sections 2.1, 2.4

MBD (Masters in Business Design)

The Masters in Business Design is an emerging and experimental graduate degree concept, which combines a Masters in Industrial Design and an MBA. The Domus Academy in Milan, Italy, is the first place to offer an MBD, although the Illinois Institute of Technology's Institute of Design offers a joint MS in Industrial Design/MBA that resembles an MBD.

Section 1.5, 3.10, 11.3

New Pragmatism

David Blood and John Doerr (of Kleiner Perkins venture capital group) have begun to put their money where their hearts are. Along with Al Gore, who has recently joined Kleiner Perkins, they have begun to invest heavily in green businesses of various types. They are interested in putting money behind the technologies and organizations that can help to make businesses more sustainable for the human communities they are part of. This social idealism, traditionally associated with the political left, is being acted upon in the business context. Innocent Drinks, Virgin Group, Whole Foods and many other firms see their work this way as well. They do not see a conflict between making money and trying to make the world a better place. New Pragmatists are pro-business individuals who believe that the world of business is just as, if not more, capable of effecting meaningful social and environmental change than are governments.

Sections 1.3, 6.6, 7.10, 11.1

Pattern Languages

This is the term that Christopher Alexander uses to describe the behaviours, use-patterns, and use-values that occur and reoccur in a given organization and its space. It is a term that is akin to the idea of culture. The repeating use-patterns that predominate in an organization define the commitments, values and culture of that organization. Pattern languages can also be referred to as the 'cultural architecture' of the organization: where behaviour and the built environment intersect.

Sections 2.4, 5.6, 8.7, 9.5

T-Shaped Recruits

Tim Brown, CEO of IDEO, talks about the importance of T-shaped employees at IDEO. These are people whose vertical axis is a hard skill (e.g. systems engineering, industrial design, graphic art, architecture, etc.) and whose horizontal axis is market empathy, cultural understanding and anthropological thinking. On one hand, T-shaped workers are interested in and understand the external cultural environment of the marketplace, while on the other, they are hands-on doers who can build and give form to new products and services that arise from consumer culture.

Sections 1.6, 3.7, 3.10

Theory X

Theory X is one of two opposing views of workplace motivation written about by Douglas McGregor, formerly of MIT's Sloan School of Management. It is the idea that the average employee generally dislikes work, is lazy and childish and must be motivated by extrinsic rewards and sanctions. It implies that, because employees are not naturally motivated and cannot be easily trusted, management must be heavy handed in implementing controls and introducing closely monitored reporting systems.

Chapter 11; Section 7.8

Theory Y

The opposite of Theory X, McGregor's Theory Y suggests that people *do* like work and working, as long as the purpose and meaning of the work is clear. If given autonomy and a sense of responsibility, employees can be trusted to take the initiative and exceed expectations. Theory Y assumes the need for less control and looser systems of reporting. The innovative firms discussed in this book lean much more heavily towards a Theory Y view of work and management than to a Theory X view.

Chapter 11; Section 7.8

Thousand Flowers Innovating

The metaphor of *a thousand flowers innovating* (derived from the Chinese Communist Party's Hundred Flowers Blooming campaign of 1956) is used here to refer to organizations where innovation is encouraged at all levels in work processes and/or company product and service offerings. At firms such as BMW, Whole Foods, W.L. Gore and Google, for example, innovation can come from anywhere, from any level of the corporate hierarchy.

Sections 1.2, 2.1, 5.5

Timeless Way of Building

A foundational idea in the architectural philosophy of Christopher Alexander is his concept of a timeless way of building. According to Alexander, universal human behaviours are observable in the way people naturally interact, communicate, live and work within built environments. A built environment includes space and spatial relationships, lighting, etc. From a Navajo hogan to a Norman Foster office building, all built spaces either do or do not align with these basic human instincts and needs and therefore either do or do not conform to a timeless way of building.

Sections 2.1, 11.1

Virtuous Spiral Organization

USC Professor Edward Lawler suggests that companies where employees are treated humanely and with dignity are not only better places to work but also often outperform companies that treat employees poorly. He talks of a virtuous spiral, wherein the better employees are treated, the more discretionary effort they will put in and, thus, the better the company will perform financially. Virtual spiral organizations are similar to the concept of human-centred enterprises.

Sections 2.1, 2.3, 5.6, 6.4, 7.8, 7.10, 8.7, 9.3, 9.5

20 Per Cent Time

At Google, full-time employees are given one day a week (or 20 per cent of their time) to work on an innovation project of their own choosing. Many of Google's new product/ service launches come from the Google labs that are formed around 20 per cent time projects. The company W.L. Gore allows its employees 10 per cent of their time for the same purpose. This not only encourages numerous new ideas to be explored, but it is also a tangible ideas-to-action mechanism where groups of employees can run with a new idea and test its commercial application. Googlers often cite 20 per cent time as one of the most compelling elements of work life at Google. It is thus a source of both new money-making innovations and an HR strategy for keeping smart and energized employees at the company.

Sections 1.6, 8.4, 8.5

Notes

Section

1.1   Jena McGregor. 'The World's Most Innovative Companies: The Leaders in Nurturing Cultures of Creativity', *Business Week Online,* 4 May 2007. Available from: http://www.businessweek.com/innovate/content/may2007/ id20070504_051674.htm?chan=search [accessed 14 January 2008].

1.1   David A. Garvin and Lynne C. Levesque. 'Meeting the Challenge of Corporate Entrepreneurship', in *Harvard Business Review*, October 2006, p. 104.

1.2   Tom Kelley. *The Ten Faces of Innovation*. New York: Currency Doubleday, 2005.

1.2   Gail Edmondson. 'BMW's Dream Factory: Sharing the wealth, listening to even the lowest-ranking workers, and rewarding risk have paid off big time', *Business Week Online*, 16 October 2006. Available from: http://businessweek. com/magazine/content/06_42/b4005072.htm [accessed 14 January 2008].

1.3   Christopher Locke, Rick Levine, Doc Searls and David Weinberger. *The Cluetrain Manifesto: The End of Business as Usual.* New York: Perseus Books, 2001.

1.3   Jim Collins. 'Foreward', in *Fast Company's Greatest Hits*, eds Mark Vamos and David Lidsky. New York: Portfolio, 2006, p. xvii.

1.4   Peter Drucker. *Management: Tasks, Responsibilities, Practices*. New York: Harper Business, 1973, pp. 61-64.

1.5   Tim Brown. 'Strategy by Design', *Fast Company Online*, June 2005, Issue 95. Available from: http://www.fastcompany.com/magazine/95/design-strategy. html [accessed 14 January 2008].

1.6   Peter Drucker. 'Rotman School of Management Advertisement', in *Fast Company*, June 2007, p. 103.

1.6   Roger Martin. 'The Design of Business', in *Rotman Magazine*, Winter 2004, pp. 7-11.

1.6   T. Brown, June 2005.

2.1   Stanton Marris Consulting. *Energizing the Organization: Meaningful Engagement,* Number 10, 2007, p. 3.

2.1   Christopher Alexander. *Timeless Way of Building.* New York: Oxford University Press, 1979, p. 25.

2.2   Richard Florida and Jim Goodnight. 'Managing for Creativity', in *Harvard Business Review*, July-August 2005, p. 128.

2.2   Charles Fishman 'Sanity Inc.', *Fast Company Online*, Issue 21, December 1998, p. 3. Available from: http://www.fastcompany.com/magazine/21/sanity_Printer_Friendly.html [accessed 14 January 2008].

2.2   C. Alexander 1979, p. 107.

2.2   Jeffrey Gangemi. 'Teaching the Benefits of Balance', *Business Week Online*, 20 September 2005. Available from: http://www.businessweek.com/bschools/content/sep2005/bs20050920_2205_bs001.htm [accessed 14 January 2008].

2.2   *Fortune's* '100 Best Companies to Work For' list, for 10 consecutive years. Available from: http://money.cnn.com/magazines/fortune/bestcompanies/full_list/ [accessed 14 January 2008].

2.2   Edward E. Lawler. 'Leading a Virtuous-Spiral Organization', in *Leader to Leader*, No. 32, Spring 2004.

2.2   Jeffrey Pfeffer. 'Breaking Through Excuses: Most Managers are good at explaining why something can't be done. Don't be one of them', *Business 2.0 Online*, 1 May 2005, p. 1. Available from: http://money.cnn.com/magazines/business2/business2_archive/2005/05/01/8259699/index.htm [accessed 14 January 2008].

3.1   Philippe Picaud. 'Leadership Forum: Why Design is not an Added Value', in Design Management Institute's *Tenth European International Design Management Conference Proceedings,* 29-31 March 2006.

3.2   Bruce Nussbaum. 'Redesigning American Business', *Business Week Online*, 29 November 2004. p. 1. Available from: http://www.businessweek.com/bwdaily/dnflash/nov2004/nf20041129_2629.htm [accessed 14 January 2008].

3.2   Barry Jaruzelski, Kevin Dehoff and Rakesh Bordia. 'Money Isn't Everything: The Booz Allen Hamilton Global Innovation 1000', *Strategy & Business* [online], Winter 2005. Available from: http://www.strategy-business.com/press/article/05406 [accessed 14 January 2008].

3.2   Jena McGregor. 'The World's Most Innovative Companies', *Business Week Online,* 24 April 2006, p. 2. Available from: http://www.businessweek.com/innovate/content/may2007/id20070504_051674.htm?chan=search [accessed 14 January 2008].

3.2   Diane Brady. 'The Immelt Revolution: He's turning CE's culture upside down, demanding far more risk and innovation', *Business Week Online*, 28 March 2005, p. 2. Available from: http://www.businessweek.com/magazine/content/05_13/b3926088_mz056.htm?chan=search [accessed 14 January 2008].

3.3   Patricia O'Connell. 'Bringing Innovation to the Home of Six Sigma: An Interview with Jeffrey Immelt', *Business Week Online*, 1 August 2005, p. 1. Available from: http://www.businessweek.com/magazine/content/05_31/b3945409.htm?chan=search [accessed 14 January 2008].

3.3   Bruce Nussbaum. 'The Power of Design', *Business Week Online*, 17 May 2004. p. 3. Available from: http://www.businessweek.com/magazine/content/04_20/b3883001_mz001.htm?chan=search [accessed 14 January 2008].

3.4   B. Nussbaum 2004, p. 3.

3.4   C.K. Prahalad. 'The Innovation Sandbox', in *Strategy & Business*, Autumn 2006 and 'The Fortune at the Bottom of the Pyramid', in *Strategy & Business*, First Quarter 2002.

3.4   T. Brown 2005, p. 2.

3.4   Bruce Nussbaum. 'Get Creative: How to Build Innovative Companies', *Business Week Online*, 1 August 2005, p. 3. Available from: http://www.businessweek.com/magazine/content/05_31/b3945401.htm?chan=search [accessed 14 January 2008].

3.4   Nancy Einhart. 'Clean Sweep of the Market: How P&G's Swiffer Inspired a Nation of Neat Freaks', *CNNMoney.com* [online], 1 March 2003, p. 1. Available from: http://money.cnn.com/magazines/business2/business2_archive/2003/03/01/338108/ [accessed 14 January 2008].

3.4   Larry Huston and Nabil Sakkab. 'Connect and Develop: Inside Procter and Gamble's New Model of Innovation', in *Harvard Business Review*, 1 March 2006.

3.4   Robert Berner. 'P&G's Quest for 'Wow' Design', *Business Week Online*, 1 August 2005, p. 1. Available from: http://www.businessweek.com/magazine/content/05_31/b3945423.htm?chan=search [accessed 14 January 2008].

3.5   Ian Wylie. 'Talk to Our Customers? Are You Crazy?', *Fast Company Online,* Issue 107, July 2006. Available from: http://www.fastcompany.com/magazine/107/business-at-its-best.html [accessed 14 January 2008].

3.6   Business Week. 'Keep the Change: Bank of America Case Study', *Business Week Online*, 19 June 2006. Available from: http://www.businessweek.com/magazine/content/06_25/b3989445.htm [accessed 14 January 2008].

3.7   Robert Berner. 'Design Visionary: Patrick Whitney is out to bridge the chasm between the cultures of business and design', *Business Week Online*, 19 June 2006. Available from: http://www.businessweek.com/magazine/content/06_25/b3989416.htm?chan=search [accessed 14 January 2008].

3.7   Jesse Hempel and Aili McConnon. 'The Talent Hunt: Desperate to innovate, companies are turning to design schools for nimble, creative thinkers', *Business Week Online*, 9 October 2006. p. 1-2. Available from: http://www.businessweek.com/magazine/content/06_41/b4004401.htm?chan=search [accessed 14 January 2008].

3.8   Business Week. 'Design's New School of Thought: Interview With David Kelley', *Business Week Online*, 1 August 2005, pp. 1-2. Available from: http://www.businessweek.com/magazine/content/05_31/b3945421.htm?chan=search [accessed 14 January 2008].

3.9   R. Berner 2006, p. 1.

3.10   Roger Martin. 'The Design of Business', in *Rotman Magazine*, Winter 2004.

4.1   Kate A. Kane. 'Anthropologists Go Native in the Corporate Village', *Fast Company Online,* Issue 5, October 1996. Available from: http://www. businessweek.com/magazine/content/05_31/b3945421.htm?chan=search [accessed 14 January 2008].

4.1   Spencer E. Ante. 'The Science of Desire', *Business Week Online,* 5 June 2006, p. 2. Available from: http://www.businessweek.com/magazine/content/06_23/ b3987083.htm [accessed 14 January 2008].

4.1   Bruce Nussbaum. 'Ethnography is the New Core Competence', *Business Week Online*, 19 June 2006, p. 1. Available from: http://www.businessweek.com/ magazine/content/06_25/b3989414.htm?chan=search [accessed 14 January 2008].

4.2   Genevieve Bell. 'Looking Across the Atlantic', in *Intel Technology Journal*, 3rd Quarter 2001, p. 1.

4.2   Intel. 'The Role of Ethnographic Research in Driving Technology Innovation: Lessons from Inside Asia', *Research at Intel* [online]. Available from: http:// www.intel.com/research/print/overview_insideasia_lessons.pdf [accessed 22 January 2008].

4.2   Business Week. 'It Takes a Village' [On Intel Ethnographer Tony Salvador], *Business Week Online,* 5 June 2006. Available from: http://images. businessweek.com/ss/06/05/ethnography/source/4.htm [accessed 14 January 2008].

4.3   Richard McGill Murphy. 'Getting to Know You: Microsoft Dispatches anthropologists into the field to study small businesses like yours', *Fortune Small Business Online*, 1 June 2005. Available from: http://money.cnn.com/ magazines/fsb/fsb_archive/2005/06/01/8261971/index.htm [accessed 14 January 2008].

4.3   Microsoft PressPass. 'Making Technology Correspond to People's Lives' [An Interview with Tracey Lovejoy], *Microsoft PressPass Reports*, 4 April 2005, p. 1. Available from: http://microsoft.com/presspass/features/2005/apr05/04-04Ethnographer.mspx [accessed 14 January 2008].

4.3   Tom Kelley. *The Ten Faces of Innovation*, New York: Currency Doubleday, 2005, p. 16.

4.3   Microsoft PressPass 2005, p. 2.

4.3   Microsoft Research-India. ' Technology for Emerging Markets: Projects',
        Microsoft Research [online]. Available from: http://research.microsoft.com/
        research/tem/ [accessed 14 January 2008].

4.3   C.K. Prahalad. 'The Fortune at the Bottom of the Pyramid', *Strategy &
        Business* [online], 1st Quarter 2002. Available from: http://www.strategy-
        business.com/press/article/11518?pg=0 [accessed 14 January 2008].

4.4   EPIC websites. Available from: www.epic2005.com, www.epic2006.com,
        www.epic2007.com www. [accessed 14 January 2008].

4.6   Spencer E. Ante. 'The Science of Desire: As more companies refocus squarely
        on the consumer, ethnography and its proponents have become start players',
        Business Week Online, 5 June 2006, p. 1. Available from: http://www.
        businessweek.com/magazine/content/06_23/b3987083.htm?chan=search
        [accessed 14 January 2008].

4.6   Shelly Strom. 'Ziba puts design focus into Chinese Computers', *The Portland
        Business Journal* [online], 11 March 2005, p. 2. Available from: http://www.
        ziba.com/pdfs/press/N0503_BJ_China.pdf [accessed 14 January 2008].

5.1   Kevin Freiberg and Jackie Freiberg. *Nuts!: Southwest Airlines' Crazy Recipe
        for Business and Personal Success.* New York: Broadway Books, 1996.

5.1   Jody Hoffer Gittell. *The Southwest Airlines Way: Using the Power of
        Relationships to Achieve High Performance.* New York: McGraw-Hill, 2005,
        p. 3.

5.1   Chuck Lucier. 'Herb Kelleher: The Thought Leader Interview', *Strategy &
        Business* [online], Summer 2004, pp. 1-2. Available from: http://www.strategy-
        business.com/press/article/04212?pg=0 [accessed 14 January 2008].

5.2   J. Gittell 2005.

5.3   J. Gittell 2005.

5.3   Peter Carbonara. 'Hire For Attitude, Train for Skill', *Fast Company Online*,
        Issue 04, August 1996. Available from: http://fastcompany.com/magazine/04/
        hiring_Printer_Friendly.html [accessed 14 January 2008].

5.4   J. Gittell 2005, p. 89.

5.4   K. Freiberg and J. Freiber 1996.

5.5   K. Freiberg and J. Freiber 1996.

5.5   Herb Kelleher. 'A Culture of Commitment', *Leader to Leader* [online], No. 4, Spring 1997, p. 2. Available from: http://www.leadertoleader.org/ knowledgecenter/journal.aspx?ArticleID=143 [accessed 14 January 2008].

5.5   Nirmalya Kumar. 'Strategies to Fight Low-cost Rivals', in *Harvard Business Review*, December 2006.

5.5   J. Gittell 2005, p. 57.

5.6   K. Freiberg and J. Freiber 1996.

5.6   Christopher Alexander. *The Order of Nature: An Essay on the Art of Building and the Nature of the Universe.* Berkeley, CA: Centre for Environmental Structure, 2002, p. 46.

5.6   J. Gittell, p. 14.

5.6   J. Collins 2006, pp. xvii-xviii.

6.1   David Brooks. *Bobos in Paradise: The New Upper Class and How They Got There.* New York: Simon & Schuster, 2001.

6.1   Whole Foods Market Inc. (WFMI) at *Yahoo Finance* [online]. Available from: http://finance.yahoo.com/q?s=wfmi [accessed 14 January 2008].

6.2   Bruce Horovitz. 'A whole new ballgame in grocery shopping', *USA Today* [online], 8 March 2005, p. 1. Available from: http://www.usatoday.com/ money/industries/food/2005-03-08-wholefoods-cover-usat_x.htm [accessed 14 January 2008].

6.3   Conifer Research. 'How to Find Buried Treasures Using Experience Maps', *Conifer Research* [online], 2002. Available from: http://www.coniferresearch. com/pdf/ConiferExperienceMaps.pdf [accessed 14 January 2008].

6.3   B. Horowitz 2005, p. 3.

6.4   Charles Fishman, 'The Anarchist's Cookbook', *Fast Company Online*, Issue 84, July 2004. Available from: http://pf.fastcompany.com/magazine/84/wholefoods.html [accessed 14 January 2008].

6.4   Charles Fishman. 'Whole Foods is all Teams', *Fast Company Online*, Issue 02, April/May 1996. Available from: http://www.fastcompany.com/magazine/02/team1.html [accessed 14 January 2008].

6.5   Lawrence Fisher. 'Ricardo Semler Won't Take Control', *Strategy & Business* [online], Winter 2005. Available from: http://www.strategy-business.com/press/article/05408?pg=0 [accessed 14 January 2008].

6.5   C. Fishman 2004.

6.6   Bruce Horovitz. 'Whole Foods goes with the wind', *USA Today Online*, 9 January 2006, p. 1. Available from: http://www.usatoday.com/money/industries/food/2006-01-09-whole-foods-usat_x.htm [accessed 14 January 2008].

6.6   Austin Business Journal. 'Whole Foods pledges $10M to support small farms', *Austin Business Journal* [online], 3 July 2006. Available from: http://austin.bizjournals.com/austin/stories/2006/07/03/daily7.html?t=printable [accessed 14 January 2008].

7.1   Mark Pendergrast. *Uncommon Grounds: The History of Coffee and How it Transformed Our World*. New York: Basic Books, 2000.

7.3   CNNMoney.com. 'Starbucks sued for trying to sink competition', *CNNMoney.com* [online], 26 September 2006. Available from: http://money.cnn.com/2006/09/26/news/companies/starbucks/index.htm [accessed 14 January 2008].

7.3   Yahoo Finance. Available from: http://finance.yahoo.com/q/ks?s=SBUX [accessed 14 January 2008].

7.4   Ranjay Gulati, Sarah Huffman and Gary Neilson. 'The Barista Principle - Starbucks and the Rise of Relational Capital', *Strategy & Business Online*, Third Quarter 2002. Available from: http://www.strategy-business.com/press/article/20534?pg=0 [accessed 14 January 2008].

7.5   Ryan Singel. 'Café 2.0: After the Gold Rush', *Wired Online*, 18 October 2005. Available from: http://www.wired.com/techbiz/media/news/2005/10/69221 [accessed 14 January 2008].

7.6   Jena McGregor. 'The World's Most Innovative Companies', *Business Week Online*, 24 April 2006. Available from: http://www.businessweek.com/magazine/content/06_17/b3981401.htm [accessed 14 January 2008].

7.6   Alison Overholt, 'Thinking Outside the Cup', *Fast Company Online*, Issue 84, July 2004, pp. 1-2. Available from: http://www.fastcompany.com/magazine/84/starbucks_1.html [accessed 14 January 2008].

7.6   Alison Overholt. 'Do You Hear What Starbucks Hears?' [Interview with Howard Schultz], *Fast Company Online,* Issue 84, July 2004, pp. 1-2. Available from: http://www.fastcompany.com/magazine/84/starbucks_schultz.html [accessed 14 January 2008].

7.6   A. Overholt. 'Thinking Outside the Cup', p. 3.

7.7   Greg Levine. 'Starbucks Inks 'Tuesdays' Author as Donald Eyes More Media', *Forbes Online,* 8 August 2006, p. 1. Available from: http://www.forbes.com/facesinthenews/2006/08/08/starbucks-tuesdays-books-cx_gl_0808autofacescan05.html [accessed 14 January 2008].

7.7   Ronald Grover. 'Starbucks Perks Up Socially Conscious Films', *Business Week Online,* 26 April 2006, p. 1. Available from: http://www.businessweek.com/bwdaily/dnflash/apr2006/nf20060426_2414_db011.htm [accessed 14 January 2008].

7.8   R. Gulati, S. Huffman and G. Neilson 2002, p. 3.

7.8   Douglas McGregor, *The Human Side of Enterprise.* New York; McGraw-Hill Education, 1960.

7.8   Scott S. Smith. 'Grounds for Success: Interview with Starbucks CEO Howard Schultz', *Entrepreneur* [online], May 1998, p. 1. Available from: http://findarticles.com/p/articles/mi_m0DTI/is_n5_v26/ai_20923860/print [accessed 14 January 2008].

7.8   Howard Schultz. Book Excerpts from *Pour Your Heart Into It* in *The New York Times Online*, p. 9. Available from: http://www.nytimes.com/books/first/s/schultz-pour.html [accessed 14 January 2008].

7.8   Starbucks. *Starbucks Employee Manual*. Available from: http://www.starbucks.com/aboutus/SB-YSB-US-HR.pdf [accessed 14 January 2008].

7.8   Robbi Hess. 'Review of *The Starbucks Experience* by Joseph Michelli', *Business Strategies Magazine* [online], April 2007. Available from: http://www.starbucksexperience.net/media.html [accessed 14 January 2008].

7.9   Anjani Sarma. 'Latte Everywhere', *Fast Company Online*, Issue 94, May 2005. Available from: http://www.fastcompany.com/magazine/94/chatter_Printer_Friendly.html [accessed 14 January 2008].

7.9   William Meyers. 'Conscience in a Cup of Coffee', *US News & World Report Online*, 31 October 2005, p. 3. Available from: http://www.usnews.com/usnews/news/articles/051031/31schultz_3.htm [accessed 14 January 2008].

7.11   Howard Schultz. 'Memo: "The commoditization of the Starbucks experience"', *Starbucks Gossip* [online], 23 February 2007. Available from: http://starbucksgossip.typepad.com/_/2007/02/starbucks_chair_2.html [accessed 14 January 2008].

8.1   Jena McGregor, 2006.

8.1   David A. Vise. *The Google Story*. New York: Pan Books, 2006, p. 50.

8.2   Marissa Ann Mayer. 'Turning Limits into Innovation' *Business Week Online*, 1 February 2006. p. 1. Available from: http://www.businessweek.com/innovate/content/jan2006/id20060131_531820.htm?chan=search [accessed 14 January 2008].

8.2   D. Vise 2006, p. 68.

8.2   Evan Carmichael. 'The Google Guys: Sergey Brin and Larry Page', *Entrepreneurs' Stories* [online], p. 7. Available from: http://www.evancarmichael.com/Famous-Entrepreneurs/645/The-Google-Guys-Sergey-Brin-and-Larry-Page.html [accessed 14 January 2008].

8.3   D. Vise 2006, p.40.

8.4   Marissa Mayer. 'Marissa Mayer's 9 Notions of Innovation', in *Business Week's IN* [*Inside Innovation* insert], June 2006, p.11.

8.5   D. Vise, 2006.

8.5   Simon London. 'Google's random genius is no accidental strategy. Can it last?', in *Financial Times*, 1 February 2006, p. 13.

8.6   D. Vise 2006, p. 177-180.

8.7   D. Vise 2006, p. 285.

8.7   Fortune Magazine. 'Google: The New Number One' [Fortune's Best 100 Places to Work Rankings], *Fortune Online* in *CNNMoney.com,* January 2007. Available from: http://money.cnn.com/magazines/fortune/bestcompanies/2007/ [accessed 14 January 2008].

9.1   Chip Heath and Dan Heath. 'Give 'em Something to Talk About', *Fast Company Online*, Issue 116, June 2007, p. 1. Available from: http://www.fastcompany.com/magazine/116/column-made-to-stick.html [accessed 14 January 2008].

9.2   Laura Cummings. 'Just an Innocent Business', *BBC News Online*, 9 July 2003, p. 3. Available from: http://news.bbc.co.uk/1/hi/business/3014477.stm [accessed 14 January 2008].

9.2   John Russell. 'Interview with Richard Reed', *Ethical Corporation* [online], p. 3. Available from: http://www.ethicalcorp.com/content.asp?ContentID=4932 [accessed 14 January 2008].

9.3   Design Council Case Study. 'Innocent Drinks: Creative culture strengthens brand values and drives profits', *Design Council* [online], p. 1. Available from: http://www.designcouncil.org.uk/en/Case-Studies/All-Case-Studies/Innocent-Smoothies/ [accessed 14 January 2008].

9.3   Design Council Case Study. 'Innocent Drinks: Sustaining a creative culture', *Design Council* [online], p. 1. Available from: http://www.designcouncil.org.uk/en/Case-Studies/All-Case-Studies/Innocent-Smoothies/Sustaining-a-creative-culture/ [accessed 14 January 2008].

9.3   John Russell, p. 3.

9.4   Design Council Case Study. 'Innocent Drinks: Creative culture', *Design Council* [online]. Available from: http://www.designcouncil.org.uk/en/Case-Studies/All-Case-Studies/Innocent-Smoothies/ [accessed 14 January 2008].

9.4   L. Cummings 2003, p. 3.

9.4   Adam Nicolson. 'Flying to Arcadia', in *Financial Times 'Life & Arts'*, 7-8 July 2007, p. 2.

9.5   Wikipedia. 'Innocent Drinks' Entry, *Wikipedia* [online]. Available from: http://en.wikipedia.org/wiki/Innocent_Drinks [accessed 14 January 2008].

10.2   Jesse Hempel. 'Designed in China', *Business Week Online*, 9 October 2006, p. 1. Available from: http://www.businessweek.com/magazine/content/06_41/b4004412.htm?chan=search [accessed 14 January 2008].

10.2   Reena Jana. 'China Goes Luxury', *Business Week Online*, 1 December 2005, p. 2. Available from: http://www.businessweek.com/print/innovate/content/nov2005/id20051130_575911.htm [accessed 14 January 2008].

10.2   Linda Tischler. 'The Gucci Killers', *Fast Company Online,* Issue 102, January 2006. Available from: http://www.fastcompany.com/magazine/102/shanghai_Printer_Friendly.html [accessed 14 January 2008].

10.3   L. Tischler 2006, p.4.

10.3   Stephen Crane. 'This Year's Model', *CFOAsia.com*, July-August 1999, p. 4. Available from: http://www.cfoasia.com/archives/9907-24.htm [accessed 14 January 2008].

11.1   Douglas McGregor. *The Human Side of Enterprise*. New York: McGraw-Hill Education, 1960, p. 33.

11.2   Ed. Richard Boland and Frank Collopy. *Managing as Designing*. Palo Alto, CA: Stanford Business Books, 2004, pp. 7-8.

11.2   Herbert Simon. *Models of Bounded Rationality*. Cambridge, MA: MIT Press, 1984.

11.2   Boland and Collopy 2004, p. 8.

11.2   Herbert Simon, quoted in Collopy and Boland 2004, p. 8. (From *The Sciences of the Artificial,* 3rd ed. Cambridge, MA: MIT Press, 1996.)

11.4   Ricardo Semler. *The Seven Day Weekend.* New York: Arrow Books, 2003.

11.4   Stanton Marris. *Energizing the Organization: Decluttering*, Issue 5, October 2003, p. 5.

11.4   M. Evelin Ascalon, Ellen Van Velsor and Meena Wilson. 'CCL Europe Impact Study', in *Centre for Creative Leadership,* March 2004.

About Triarchy Press

Triarchy Press is an independent publishing house that looks at how organizations work and how to make them work better. We present challenging perspectives on organizations in short and pithy, but rigorously argued, books.

Through our books, viewpoints, e-publications and discussion area, we aim to stimulate ideas by encouraging real debate about organizations in partnership with people who work in them, research them or just like to think about them.

Please tell us what you think about the ideas in this book. Join the discussion at:
www.triarchypress.com/telluswhatyouthink

If you feel inspired to write - or have already written - an article, a viewpoint or a book on any aspect of organizational theory or practice, we'd like to hear from you.
Submit a proposal at:
www.triarchypress.com/writefor us

www.triarchypress.com
info@triarchypress.com

About the Author

Andrew Jones trained as a cultural anthropologist, receiving his PhD in 1997 from the University of Wisconsin-Madison. For the past ten years he has been a university lecturer and organizational consultant to businesses in the US and the UK. He taught anthropology, management and organizational behaviour at the University of Alabama, Birmingham for many years. More recently, he has been Lecturer in Leadership in the Department of Management Learning and Leadership at Lancaster University Management School in the UK.

He has consulted with companies in the food and beverage industry, construction and building, executive education, software, for-profit education and sports management. He currently works with the innovation agency, Aquifer Design, which develops tools and technologies for innovation, and with the innovation practice at Mettle Group. Mettle Group, which has offices in Sydney, Melbourne and London, is an organizational consultancy that helps companies to align strategy with culture and leadership. He is also Visiting Lecturer in Innovation and Leadership at Lancaster University Management School. He is based in Austin, Texas.

He has published articles in *Leadership, Culture & Organization, Organizational Dynamics, Human Organization, Top Consultant* and *Professional Manager Magazine*. This is his first book.

Printed in the United Kingdom
by Lightning Source UK Ltd.
127421UK00001B/1-74/P